Bioinformation

Resources Series

Bioinformation

BRONWYN PARRY AND
BETH GREENHOUGH

polity

First published in 2018 by Polity Press

Polity Press
65 Bridge Street
Cambridge CB2 1UR, UK

Polity Press
101 Station Landing, Suite 300
Medford, MA 02155, USA

ISBN-13: 978-1-5095-0545-6
ISBN-13: 978-1-5095-0546-3(pb)

A catalogue record for this book is available from the British Library.

Library of Congress Cataloging-in-Publication Data

Names: Parry, Bronwyn, author. | Greenhough, Beth, author.
Title: Bioinformation / Bronwyn Parry, Beth Greenhough.
Description: 1 | Cambridge, UK ; Malden, MA : Polity, 2017. | Series:
    Resources | Includes bibliographical references and index.
Identifiers: LCCN 2017014229 (print) | LCCN 2017031884 (ebook) | ISBN
    9781509505487 (Mobi) | ISBN 9781509505494 (Epub) | ISBN 9781509505456
    (hardback) | ISBN 9781509505463 (paperback)
Subjects: LCSH: Bioinformatics. | Biology--Data processing. | BISAC:
    POLITICAL SCIENCE / International Relations / Trade & Tariffs.
Classification: LCC QH324.2 (ebook) | LCC QH324.2 .P38 2017 (print) | DDC
    570.285--dc23
LC record available at https://lccn.loc.gov/2017014229

Typeset in 10.5 on 13pt Scala by
Servis Filmsetting Ltd, Stockport, Cheshire
Printed and bound in the UK by Clays Ltd, St Ives PLC

For further information on Polity, visit our website:
politybooks.com

Contents

Acknowledgements

We would like to thank all those who have contributed to ongoing discussions over the years on the nature of bioinformation, its emerging markets and the social, ethical and legal implications of its use as a resource in contemporary society. These include: Barbara Prainsack, Catherine Waldby, Kaushik Sunder Rajan, Nik Rose, Jenny Reardon, Gail Davies, Emma Roe, Catherine Nash, Klaus Hoeyer, Chris Philo, Sarah Whatmore, Mary Ebeling, Nick Bingham, Lochlann Jain, Steve Hinchliffe, Tim Brown and Jamie Lorimer. We have benefited tremendously from your insights, which have really helped to refine our thinking on this complex issue. Our wonderful editors at Polity, Louise Knight and Nekane Tanaka Galdos, have been so encouraging, supportive and patient, and we remain indebted to them for their creative commissioning of this work and careful stewardship to completion. Colleagues in our respective Departments of Global Health and Social Medicine at King's College London, and Geography and the Environment at Oxford have been equally generous in their support of this project. We are very grateful to Keble College, Oxford for providing a visiting fellowship for Bronwyn that first helped us get this project off the ground. Katya Baker provided invaluable research assistance throughout, for which we give our sincere thanks.

Lastly, Bronwyn would like to thank her family – Sally, Alex and Jacob – for their unending love and for ever so patiently providing the time and space needed to conceptualize, research and write this book. She would also like to thank Beth for being such a brilliant collaborator and Andy for helping her to find time away from her young family to work on this project. Beth would like to thank Karl Benediktsson from the University of Iceland and all those who supported, participated in and contributed to her early doctoral work on Iceland's Health Sector Database. She would like to thank Bronwyn for inviting her to be involved in this project and putting up with her erratic contributions during maternity leave. Last, but by no means least, Beth is very grateful to Andy, Molly and Fergus for allowing her the time and space to realize this work.

Abbreviations

ANTHC	Alaska Native Tribal Health Consortium
CBD	Convention on Biological Diversity
CCTV	close circuit television
CDC	Centre for Disease Control and Prevention (US)
cDNA	complementary DNA
CEPH	Centre d'étude du polymorphisme humain (France)
CF	cystic fibrosis
CFS	chronic fatigue syndrome
DNA	deoxyribonucleic acid
EGP	Estonian Genome Project
EPIC	European Prospective Investigation into Cancer and Nutrition
FAO	Food and Agriculture Organization of the United Nations
FDA	Food and Drug Administration (US)
FOSS	free and open source software
gDNA	genomic DNA
GWAS	genome-wide association studies
HGDP	Human Genome Diversity Project
HIPAA	Health Insurance Portability and Accountability Act (US)
HMP	Human Microbiome Project
HRT	hormone replacement therapy
HTLV	human T-lymphotrophic virus
HUGO	Human Genome Organisation

HUNT	Nord-Trøndelag Health Study (Norway)
HSCIC	Health and Social Care Information Centre (UK)
HSD	Health Sector Database (Iceland)
NCBI	National Centre for Biotechnology Information (US)
NHS	National Health Service (UK)
NICE	National Institute of Health and Clinical Excellence
NIH	National Institute of Health (US)
ME	myalgic encephalomyelitis
MOOM	Massive Open Online Medicine
PKU	phenylketonuria
P3G	Public Population Project in Genomics
RAFI	Rural Advancement Foundation International
RNA	ribonucleic acid
SNPs	single nucleotide polymorphisms
SRA	Sequence Read Archive
TMS	Tandem Mass Spectrometry
TRIPS	Trade Related Intellectual Property Rights
UK	United Kingdom
US	United States
WTO	World Trade Organization

CHAPTER ONE

Genesis:
What is Bioinformation?

Introduction

On 17 November 1903, the *London Daily News* led with an important crime story with the title *Jewel Haul Sequel: The Fingerprint Clue*.[1] Contained within the report was a description of the arrest of one Henry Elliot, aged 26, on suspicion of the robbery of jewellery worth an estimated £5,000 from the auction house of Messrs. Knight, Frank and Rutley of Conduit Street. Arrested as he lay in his bed, Elliot denied the charges, asserting boldly, 'That's a lie!'. Chief Inspector Drew assured him it was not – that his presence at the scene had been established by the detection of 'traces of finger marks' that, when sent to Scotland Yard's newly formed Finger-Mark Impression Department, were confirmed as Elliot's very own. A search of his lodgings, which revealed the hoard, served to seal his fate. Although the article offers no account of it, we cannot but wonder what Elliot must have thought about this new technique that had turned his own body into a traitorous witness of his nefarious activities. How was it possible that information about his identity and his whereabouts could have been divined from mere fragments of his bodily material shed miles away from his home? What other information about his fate might be similarly derived?

The science of fingerprint identification was then still in its infancy, and its success relied on an allied technique of anthropometric classification developed in France in 1879 by Parisian police officer Alphonse Bertillon. Bertillon came from a family of notable statisticians and demographers, and he shared their interests in statistical probability, measurement and systems of classification, believing that they could be brought to bear in improving criminal identification. Drawing on these techniques, he devised a system of physical measurements of the head and body and notation of individual markings such as tattoos and scars. These measurements were entered onto cards and accompanied with a photographic portrait – the image that we now know as 'the mug shot' – that was used to create a unique descriptor and record of the offender.

These cards were then systematically filed and cross-indexed so that they could be easily retrieved. The utility of this new system of anthropomorphic identification was immediately evident to commentators of the day. As one journalist for the *Standard* newspaper astutely noted: '[B]y taking the measurements of a person it becomes possible to ascertain his identity even if he is already included in the records under *any name whatever* ... [T]he highly ingenious mode of classification by which the cards are deposited in a cabinet is the most admirable part of the system, providing, as it does, a ready and perfect means of reference amongst many thousands of records.'[2] However, Bertillon's method of obtaining these physical measurements was rather laborious to perform, requiring specialized technical equipment that needed to be constantly recalibrated. By harnessing it to eugenicist Francis Galton's emergent, much more efficient method of finger printing, an exceptionally powerful new technology was born for divining information about individuals – their identity, experiences and fate – from their own bodily materials.[3]

Molecular Biology and Bioinformational Metaphors

This enterprise was not, however, confined solely to the world of criminal activity and what was later to become forensic science. The question of how an individual's physiology could inform understandings of their life experience was, at virtually the same historical moment, also beginning to preoccupy those working in the new discipline of molecular biology. As the century progressed, a series of key breakthroughs improved understanding of genetic disease. The rediscovery of Mendel's laws of hereditary inheritance, Avery's discovery that genes are made up of DNA, and Watson, Crick and Franklin's later elucidation of DNA's double helical structure all allowed scientists to begin explicating the primary relationships and mechanisms that guide biological replication and function. A key set of questions animated much of this research. How do genotypes (the specific genetic make-up of individuals) affect phenotypes (the observable characteristics of that individual)? Are phenotypes genetically predetermined or can they be shaped by environmental interactions? How are biological messages or 'instructions' conveyed within an organism?

In order to find concepts and language capable of capturing the complexities of these processes, scientists drew on a number of metaphors that were popular at the time in the fields of cybernetics and communication theory. They began to describe DNA as containing genetic 'code' that signals to cells how they should operate or behave. This idea that biological material could contain information that directs the function of the organism was further cemented by the fact that this genetic code was signified by the letters of DNA's four nucleotide bases: adenine, cytosine, guanine and thymine. The resultant strings of letters (ACGT) that are used to describe particular sequences of DNA thus appear as a kind of language or expressed information. Much debate later ensued over whether DNA was actually a form of information or whether it simply acted as a means of conveying biological instructions that we like to characterize as 'information'.[4] Although that question has not, and perhaps will never be, fully resolved, it is clear that informational metaphors such as 'transcription', 'translation', 'coding for' and 'scripting' have since become very popular and powerful tropes for describing the genetic mechanisms and outputs that shape all of biological life. Use of the term 'bioinformation', which first entered public debate and reportage during the 1980s, has grown exponentially since then. It remains, however, a term that is, in many respects, rather poorly defined. So what exactly is 'bioinformation'?

What is Bioinformation?

A casual perusal of the internet reveals the many ways in which the term bioinformation is currently employed. It has been used to refer to DNA sequences stored on computer databases, archived pathological samples, biomedical records, the results of clinical trials and even pharmaceutical consumption patterns. Other references are made to 'genetic information'. This is defined as information derived from an individual's genetic tests, or from genetic tests taken by their family members, and can include information about the manifestation of a disease or disorder in that family's medical history. Bioinformation has also been used to describe information obtained from forensic and medical examinations, such as that contained in reports and notes documented in patient and criminal records. Yet another important form of bioinformation is ecological data derived from observational or field studies of human, animal, plant or microbial populations that provides information on habitats, prevalence and incidence of disease, mortality and the like.

It might seem, at first glance, that there are basically two kinds of bioinformation; the first we could think of as derivative, the second as descriptive. 'Derivative' bioinformation appears to be the kind that is *derived* directly from the organism or the individual DNA sequence information, for example. The second, 'descriptive' bioinformation, might be thought to include forms of information that we use to *describe* the biology of individuals and their way of life: information about their response to their environment, experience of disease, risk of mortality or social identity, for example. These two kinds of bioinformation seem to exist in two distinct registers: the first (DNA embedded in tissues) seems 'fleshier', the latter (such as medical records) 'wordier'. The resources that Polity has, to date, focused on in the series of which this book is one, such as coffee, gold or food, seem to be much less complicated entities, existing simply as physical goods that are traded as such in formal marketplaces. Their identities seem, in this respect at least, to be much more fixed: they are what they are. Bioinformation proves much harder to pin down. One of its unique characteristics, as we shall see, is that it can exist in many different material forms and can thus operate across many different 'registers' simultaneously. First, however, we need to extract bioinformation from its source.

The bodily structure of fleshy living organisms can provide all manner of information that may have utility in scientific or social endeavours. One of the primary scientific enterprises of the latter part of the twentieth century was to develop sophisticated new technologies for making this information available to others. There were three key parts to this work. The first involved finding ways of stabilizing fleshy, corruptible tissue and presenting it in more manageable forms, such as cryogenically frozen tissue or cell lines. The second involved developing techniques for examining or 'reading' the many varieties of biological information that could be derived from such investigations. These included, for example, finding methods for analysing the genetic composition of the tissue and establishing how it reacted on exposure to different substances such as drugs; the former was enabled by DNA or RNA sequencing, the latter via high throughput screening. Other examples include methods for tracking and tracing the behaviour of populations over space and time, in particular the surveillance of those seen as presenting a threat to the state. The third involved finding ways of presenting this biological information about organisms or populations in more standardized and portable forms; for example, electronic records stored on computer databases.

This task of converting bioinformation into 'data' that can be copied and circulated electronically became the responsibility of those working in the emerging field of bioinformatics. Rapid advances in computing and information technologies gave biologists, or, more accurately, biologists and their data science collaborators, the capacity to process and begin to interpret genetic code. This in turn led to the reconfiguration of biology as a data-driven information science.[5] Much of this work has involved devising or refining techniques for computer-based storage, manipulation, modelling and visualization of what is termed 'biological data'. This is defined as data or measurements derived from the examination of biological sources that are stored or exchanged in a digital form. However, even 'biological data', so described, comprises more kinds of information than one might think. As John Wooley and Herbert Lin suggest, the information associated with a biological entity could include 'two-dimensional images, three-dimensional structures, one-dimensional sequences, annotations of these data structures, and so on'.[6]

It is enticing to imagine that bioinformation subsists a

priori, that is to say that it exists within organisms as something that is both present and determinate and simply awaiting discovery through investigation. However, as several commentators helpfully remind us, this is not the case. Information about biological organisms (including human beings) – their internal composition, structure, function, behaviour and disposition – exists, but can only be 'made available in the world' by first rendering it as data of some kind. Data, as Rob Kitchin suggests, consists of 'raw elements that can be abstracted from phenomena and measured and recorded in various ways'. However, given that these data points constitute simply *a selection* of the total sum of all the information available, they necessarily remain 'inherently partial, selective and representative'.[7]

Those who generate bioinformational data are aware that, in order for it to be widely circulated and used, it first needs to be, as philosopher of science Sabina Leonelli puts it, 'packaged' so it can 'travel beyond the boundaries of their own investigations'.[8] These data journeys prove crucial, Leonelli argues, as

> [they] don't merely affect the interpretation of the data: they determine what counts as data and for whom in the first place ... [such decisions] are made on the basis of the interests of the specific individuals involved, the materials and formats of the objects in question, the ethos of the relevant communities, existing standards of what counts as reliable data, conditions for data access and use, and shifting understandings of data ownership and value.[9]

In other words it is not possible to arrive at a 'context-independent' definition of biological data because it is always relational: *what data is depends on who uses it, how, and for what purpose.*

So what kind of a resource is bioinformation then? Is it bodily or informational, material or immaterial, private or public? Perhaps the best way to grasp its complex existence is to understand that it is neither material nor immaterial but, rather, *materialized* in different ways at different points in its existence. The question of how best to describe the biological information of interest will necessarily shape a researcher's decisions about how that information is derived and in what form it is best presented to the world. Distinctions between what is 'derivative' and what is 'descriptive' bioinformation therefore ultimately collapse as they are mutually constituted. Bioinformation may appear at different moments to be more derivative or more descriptive, fleshier or wordier, but in fact it usually exists, in any given moment, in a multiplicity of forms. An example would be information on tumours found in pathological slides.

Pathological slides (see figure 1.1) consist of finely sliced human tissue that has been stained and mounted between pieces of glass. These slides are then scanned using electron microscopes. The resultant images, which we can think of as a kind of technologized artefact of the tissue, are then digitized and numerically analysed using computer algorithms. These algorithms automate the manual counting of particular structures within the tissue, allowing the technician to detect the presence of tumours, the incidence of which is recorded in a dataset. The scan, the algorithm, the slide and the dataset all contain valuable bioinformation – it is just instantiated and thus made available in different ways, at different times and places, according to the needs of its authors and consumers. Bearing all these complexities in mind, we can nevertheless still arrive at a useful definition of this elusive resource. *Bioinformation, we suggest, is a term that refers to all information, no matter how constituted, arising from analyses of biological organisms and their behaviour, that can be used to elucidate their structure or function, identify individuals, or differentiate them from each other.* Although, as we note, valuable

Figure 1.1   Example of a pathological slide

Photograph: Ania Dabrowska, Mind Over Matter project.

Source: Parry, B. and Dabrowska, A., *Mind Over Matter: Memory, Forgetting, Brain Donation and the Search for Cures for Dementia.* Practice and Theory: London. 2011

sets of biological data can and have been constructed from ecological and environmental studies of animal, plant and microbial organisms and populations, we are, in this work, focusing primarily on the fate of bioinformation sourced from human beings.[10]

Registers of Bioinformation

Although, as we note, bioinformation can take a number of forms, this is not to say that the material instantiation that bioinformation takes is not important. In fact, the register in which bioinformation exists at any given moment plays an absolutely critical role, as we shall see, in determining who can access it, use it, circulate it, own it or capitalize on it.

To understand why this is so, it is useful to begin by exploring how the different forms that bioinformation take can shape our relationships to it. Blocks of human tissue and the pathology slides that we just discussed contain valuable bioinformation, but they also remain, in the eyes of many, identifiable 'body parts' that are endowed with all the spiritual and emotional significance associated with human remains. Others may, however, view the tissue differently, and this can dramatically alter their approach to its collection and use. In the early 2000s in Britain, a national scandal arose when the parents of children who had died at two of the country's leading hospitals, Alder Hey and Bristol, discovered that samples of their children's tissue – including whole organs – had been stored in the hospital sites for many years without their permission. Some parents had initially given consent for the material to be examined to establish cause of death, but they were outraged to learn that it had subsequently been retained for future research purposes.[11]

The children's tissue had clearly come to exist in two registers simultaneously: to the parents, it remained a precious fragment of a beloved family member whom they wished to inter with full funeral rites; to medical researchers, it constituted a rich source of diagnostic bioinformation that they could treat, more dispassionately, as a purely scientific resource. Consent issues aside, both are legitimate conceptions, although it is clear that they cannot easily be accommodated by both parties. Personalized bioinformation – that is, information that can be linked to an individual or group of individuals – is also an unusual resource for another reason. It is of interest not only to the individual from whom it is drawn, but also to that individual's kin, especially those to whom they are biologically related. This is because bioinformation can be very revelatory: it can indicate potential predisposition to genetic disease and it can be used to certify or dispute biological relatedness or substantiate or disprove racial identity; all matters that can have a direct and profound impact on the lives of the source individual and their relatives. Who, then, should be considered to be 'the owner' of this sensitive bioinformation?

The value of bioinformation stems, in part, from its ability to provide important explanations for why diseases progress as they do, and how genetics shape individuals' interactions with their environment. Enormous moral complexities thus arise when an individual refuses to share bioinformation derived from genetic tests with family members who might also be so affected. Respect for confidentiality is a firmly established tradition in medical practice, and patient–physician trust is often built on the assumption that confidentiality will be maintained at all costs. However, as bioethicists Mike Parker and Anneke Lucassen suggest, treating bioinformation as a 'personal bank account' that only one individual is able to access or control can be highly problematic, particularly if that information has the potential to shape the life experiences and chances of that person's relatives in significant ways.[12] Parker and Lucassen argue that it would be more appropriate to proceed on the assumption that genetic bioinformation is a familial resource that must be held in a 'joint account' for all relations to access equally. On this reading, bioinformation, although drawn from an individual, ought to be understood as something more akin to a communal or collective resource: one that should not, therefore, be subject to autonomous decision-making.

Taking this as a starting point, our intention here is to elucidate, using an interdisciplinary approach informed by science and technology studies, how bioinformation is abstracted from its subjects (its messy corporeal existence) and rendered as notated sequences, photographic images, x-rays, slides, or written or digitalized clinical, criminal or credit records – in short, as highly accessible, readable and manipulable distillations of bioinformation (data and aggregated big datasets) that now have tremendous commercial and economic value. In fact, as Watson suggests, drawing a direct line of connection with earlier, historical resource economies, bioinformation has become, in the twenty-first century, as valuable as oil: 'a natural resource spewing forth from each of us as we live digitally – quantifiable and monetisable'.[13] In tracing how this vital new resource travels, we explore what happens as it becomes 'footloose' and begins to circulate as a fully realized commodity that can be up-and-down-loaded, shared on peer-to-peer platforms, and circulated globally to an audience of scientific and medical consumers 24/7.

Political Economies of Bioinformation

One of the remarkable features of contemporary capitalism, as several commentators have noted, has been its interest in the project of realizing commercial value from the exploitation of 'life itself', as sociologist Nikolas Rose puts it.[14] The capitalist economy has historically sought to capture the surplus labour power of individuals, but new ventures now seek to extract value from commercializing access to biological products and processes themselves. The emergence of these new industries and their associated markets has been driven in part by the pharmaceutical industry's efforts to generate products to meet a range of conditions, including those caused by genetics, of which we are now much more aware. Other equally lucrative markets have been created, as anthropologist Kaushik Sunder Rajan and sociologist Melinda Cooper suggest, by speculating on new innovations that could potentially address future health risks via projects such as personalized medicine, even if such ventures may later prove to be based largely on 'the magic of being able to pull rabbits out of hats'.[15]

The resources on which these new bioeconomies draw include tissues, cells and parts of the body, with the latter conceived of, as sociologist Thomas Lemke puts it, 'as an informational network rather than a physical substrate or an anatomical machine'.[16] Many of these materials first enter this economy as gifts that are donated by individuals for the purposes of medical research. However, they do not remain in this particular material form or retain their uncomplicated gift status for long. As Catherine Waldby and Robert Mitchell's seminal work on bioinformational economies reminds us, the engineering of tissues after donation means that they are able to be put to a variety of uses and consequently adopt multiple trajectories: '[D]onated tissues are not simply transferred intact from one person to another, but rather diverted through laboratory processes where they may be fractionated, cloned, immortalized and multiplied in various ways [therefore] tissue sourced from one person may be distributed in altered forms along complex pathways to multiple recipients.'[17]

Neither can these new renderings of tissue, such as cell lines, DNA sequences or forensic, genetic or medical databases, be viewed, as the body part might be, as something that simply 'belongs' to an individual or family. This is because they are now, simultaneously, *technical inventions*. Enabling what was once biologically embedded and inaccessible bioinformation to exist in the world in more manageable, readable and mobile forms is a task that requires considerable investments of skill, expertise and creativity (what is known as intellectual labour) on the part of scientists, researchers and technicians. They are effectively designing new technological 'products', and, like other product designers, they wish to have their work acknowledged and to be allowed to capitalize on their inventions. One way of achieving this is for scientists (and the organizations or companies they work for) to claim these bioinformatic inventions in the courts as their 'owned' intellectual property that others must pay to access.[18] What began as a gift has segued slowly but progressively into the condition of becoming a commodity that can be bought and sold for profit. It is through this paradoxical chain of events that bioinformation has come to inhabit two identities simultaneously: the first as highly personal and private data, the other as corporately owned property.

Negotiating the dynamics of this dual identity has given rise to some deeply problematic and, as yet, still largely unresolved questions. Who should have the right to control how bioinformation is used? If the scientist or bioinformatic specialist has 'made' the artefact (e.g., the cell line, DNA sequence or database) and successfully applied for a patent on her invention, shouldn't she have the exclusive right to determine how it is used and to charge royalties for its use? But what of the unique individual from whom that information was first derived and his extended family members who share the same genetic material? Should they have the right to prohibit such uses? Or alternatively, to share in the financial rewards that arise from uses they do approve? Should rights to bioinformation be intergenerational? Should it be possible, for example, for an individual to determine how his mother's genetic information is used and by whom, even after her death?

High-profile cases such as that of Henrietta Lachs and John Moore (discussed in Chapter 3) first focused global attention on these key questions in the 1980s, but, despite the passage of time, they remain, to this day, largely unresolved. One of the key aims of this book is to generate a coherent account of how this vital new resource is being commoditized and to examine the political, social and economic implications of the global expansion of a largely unregulated trade in bioinformation. This task becomes more urgent as the number and types of consumers of bioinformation continue to proliferate, and as the quantity of bioinformation that we are generating and trading begins to grow, exponentially. Information, as many social theorists have noted, is a very unusual resource in that it is perhaps the only one that it is possible to give away and yet still own. Its ability to be replicated and circulated without diminution of the original source creates a wealth of opportunities, but also many challenges. As those working in the music and social media sectors have discovered, technologies that enable peer-to-peer sharing and global electronic distribution of informational products such as blogs, news reports, YouTube clips and music undoubtedly expand markets, but also seriously complicate the task of tracing where such products go, who profits from them and how.

Bioinformation can also now be copied with perfect fidelity, up-and-down-loaded by multiple users and disseminated instantaneously via electronic circuits into similarly expansive global networks of trade and exchange. Who could or should benefit from its commercial exploitation and how might that use compromise privacy regarding personal identity or the circulation of confidential information? Far from being a dry philosophical matter, the question of when and how bioinformation makes the leap from being a resource that lies dormant in the flesh of all beings to one that can be derived, circulated and marketed to a diverse array of global consumers is a matter of concern for anyone interested in the question of what might happen to their own bioinformation and of the implications of turning it into a commodity that can be bought and sold. Through a series of small but highly topical case studies, including the commercialization of human sequence data drawn from individuals in the West and remote indigenous communities, the forensic use of retained bioinformation, biobanking and genealogical research, this book will demonstrate how a growing demand for this resource has driven the emergence of a burgeoning new global economy in bioinformation and a big data revolution in the collection and linkage of bioinformation from many different sources.

Chapter Synopses

In chapters that follow, we use case studies to unpack and explore some of the intense contestations, political debates and concerns that have surrounded the practice of collecting and using human bioinformation – from its birth in early forensic science, to its rapid expansion in the genetic data programmes of the 1980s, to the big data revolution that we are experiencing today. In order to understand how and why bioinformation has become such a valuable commodity, as well as the political and economic implications of this new global trade, we need first to identify the factors that have made its emergence possible, and the key ethical, social, economic and political issues that have surrounded and shaped its emergence as a new industrial resource. Our intention is to chart the profound changes that are taking place in the political economy of trade in bioinformation and to explore with the reader the very significant challenges these pose for the governance of this exceptionally valuable new resource. These are addressed in detail in the following chapters, a brief outline of which is provided below.

We begin our analysis in Chapter 2 with a simple question: where does bioinformation come from? Recent advances in technology have made it possible to extract and store bioinformation from human beings in historically unprecedented ways. In order to undertake this work, it is first necessary to access and examine some kind of donated or stored tissue. But how is such tissue sourced? This proves to be an absolutely critical question that profoundly shapes how useful the bioinformation that is extracted from it will be, and how it may later be owned or used. This is, in effect, a question of provenance. Researchers are generally examining bioinformation in order to explore possible relationships between a person's biology and their health or behaviour; between say, the crime and the criminal who committed it, the diseased brain and the person's Alzheimer's, an individual's genealogy and his or her current relationships. The more that is known about an individual's current existence – in terms of genetic make-up, lifestyle, behaviour and relationships – the richer the resultant picture and analysis will be. Random samples of tissue that come without this kind of history are of relatively little worth. Knowing where (and from whom) biological data has been derived thus becomes a key determinant of what makes that resource valuable. Yet provenance is also more than this; it also encompasses questions about the wider terms and conditions under which the bioinformation was collected.

There are, broadly speaking, two routes through which large collections of human bioinformation are created: the first is through the deliberate creation of new biobanks (collections of stored human tissue, DNA samples, sequences and associated records), and the second through the repurposing of existing collections of archived tissue samples, genetic information or biological data. In this chapter, we examine how the repurposing of existing collections has become increasingly controversial, particularly when it involves allowing commercial companies to access collections that were originally created for public, nonprofit use. We also explore here how bioinformation is collected from suspect populations, those who are known or who are thought to have committed crimes, as well as those who have witnessed them. Bioinformation is usually collected from the latter with their consent, but can be taken forcibly from the former in the interests of detecting and preventing crime. We consider how this bioinformation is archived and examine what the moral and ethical implications are of retaining bioinformation from suspect populations for long periods of time, particularly in circumstances where the source individual, while a suspect, has not been convicted of a criminal act. In so doing, we also draw attention to how valuable forensic bioinformation has become to the rapidly burgeoning global surveillance industry, a matter we develop in more detail in Chapter 5. These case studies highlight some of the ethical and political complexities that surround the generation and later use of such collections of human tissue, notably the thorny issues of motivations, consent, benefit sharing and rights to privacy.

This brings us to another vital question: why do people donate their bioinformation (if they do so voluntarily)? Many donors are motivated by a wish for society to benefit from the insights and scientific breakthroughs that the large-scale, intensive analysis of collected bioinformation can bring. Yet defining what constitutes a benefit, and whether this refers simply to broad social benefits or encompasses direct financial compensation as well, is, as we shall demonstrate, a fraught issue, giving rise to intense debates over how such rewards could or should be dispersed and to whom. We also explore why some individuals might prefer not to donate, and identify some of the risks that participating in biobanking initiatives can bring. These include, for example, that sensitive bioinformation could be circulated to others without the donor's consent, or be accessed illegally, or even be requisitioned by court order. In cases where research links a study population to a particular susceptibility to disease, it is also possible that being identified as a donor (and thereby part of that study population) may even lead to direct stigmatization and discrimination.

In the past, biobank operators have sought to allay donors, fears and concerns about the risks of participation by offering assurances. They claim to be able to keep personally identifiable data associated with bioinformation – names, address and so forth – confidential, and to successfully anonymize that data for the purposes of large-scale analysis. This, however, raises a further set of questions and concerns about how best to balance a donor's right to privacy and anonymity against the need conserve that data's provenance; that is to say, to ensure that donated tissue and bioinformation can be linked back to detailed (and thus potentially identifiable) records of that individual's lived experience. That link can present a major threat to the donor's privacy, but the establishment of such linkages is vital if individuals wish to receive feedback on the findings of future tests or improve the value of future biomedical research.

Concerns over whether the donor fully understands both the costs and benefits of participation and how to communicate these effectively are key issues for those charged with responsibility for securing their informed consent to participate in biobanks. Consent, the process of giving formal permission for something to happen, is typically seen as a necessary prerequisite to obtaining or using human tissue for medical or research purposes. We discuss how the operation of consenting procedures in biobanking initiatives has proven immensely complex in practice and has been continually adapted over time. A comparative analysis of the approach to consent taken by two different national biobanks, Iceland's Health Sector Database (HSD) and the United Kingdom's national Biobank, reveals much about the difficulty of ensuring that consent is, in fact, fully informed and the problems that arise if it is not.

The Icelandic HSD was lobbied by a privately owned bio-pharmaceutical company, DeCODE Genetics; UK Biobank was created by accessing tissue and data from a wide cross section of volunteers, recruited from all echelons of British society. The lack of effective consent, despite political support, in the former case induced huge controversy, which then shaped the ways in which these issues were approached in subsequent projects, including UK Biobank. Although participants in UK Biobank were more comprehensively consulted than their Icelandic counterparts, the consents that they were asked to give were for very broad and often unspecified future uses of their bioinformation. Some scholars expressed concern that the idea of 'informed broad consent' is a contradiction in terms, making the retrospective use of bioinfomation collected under the 'broad consent' model unethical, a matter that we discuss in depth in Chapter 3.

Ensuring that data has been collected with the informed consent of donors has thus become an important determinant of bioinformatic provenance and quality. What implications does this have, then, for tissues and DNA that have been co-opted into biobanking projects through retrospective or nonvoluntary accessioning? The Human Genome Diversity Project (HGDP) here provides an interesting case in point. Although initially celebrated for creating the first genetic map of human diversity and migration, its success relied on the often poorly consented collection and analysis of genetic samples and information from many thousands of indigenous populations, characterized, rather crudely, as 'isolates of historic interest'. Drawing on Jenny Reardon's incisive critique of the use of genomic databases, we explore how these collections of bioinformation were drawn into wider genealogical enterprises that, while illuminating much about our shared ancestries, also served to characterize such populations in ways that have perpetuated and normalized, rather than alleviated, racist attitudes.

The conflicts of interest that arose between biobank donors and researchers in the HGDP raises the question of who is entitled to benefit from the exploitation of bioinformation. Chapters 3 and 4 deal with two key aspects of this question: first, how bioinformation transited from being personal data and material to being the private property of institutions and corporations (Chapter 3) and, second, how markets in bioinformation are constituted and how the gains that arise from commercialization are disbursed and shared (Chapter 4).

We open Chapter 3 by asking how it is that human bioinformation could be converted into a commodity that can be bought, sold and owned as private property. Privatization became the preferred mode of ownership of many resources from the mid-seventeenth century onwards, as common lands were enclosed and private rights of ownership were extended through land claims, mineral extraction licences, fishing rights and the like. Yet, as evidenced by the movement for the abolition of slavery within the British Empire (1772–1833), it was increasingly seen as both ethically and morally unacceptable to reduce humans and their derivatives to the status of being mere 'objects' of property law. Therefore, to many, it might seem incomprehensible that any element of an individual's body could somehow be owned by another. In this chapter, we set about explaining this troubling paradox, revealing why individual donors cannot exert ownership rights over their biological samples or bioinformation while others involved in their collection and use – researchers, biobanks and commercial biotechnology enterprises – can.

We begin by briefly examining the history of bodily commodification and exploring the economic and legal arguments that have been employed to allow some individuals to claim rights of property in the body parts of others. Many of these relate to the physical transformations that human tissue and DNA undergo as they are bought to life as industrial commodities. These include stabilizing tissue and rendering it in more technologized forms: as cell lines, genomic sequences or electronic data, for example. Each of these new products is viewed as an 'invention' that their creators (such as research scientists or computer software engineers) have effectively 'manufactured'. The courts, in recognizing the intellectual and physical labour these creators had invested in their generation, rewarded them with rights to determine how they are used and to profit from their commercialization. Owners of cell lines began to patent them, while those who 'compiled' genetic sequence databases moved to copyright them, actions that allowed both groups to set the terms and conditions of their use. It is through such mechanisms that bioinformation became commercialized, allowing the monetary value of the resource to be fully realized for the first time. It remains a very curious anomaly, however, that although rights to modified human tissue, DNA and bioinformation were established, none of these rights accrues to the individuals who first donated the tissue, the raw material of the bioinformational economy.

Having outlined the political economy of this burgeoning global market, we then pose the question: why do its creators *not* share in the benefits that accrue from the commercial exploitation of our bioinformation? Using the cases of Henrietta Lacks, John Moore and the Hagahai people of Papua New Guinea as illustrative examples, we investigate the complexities of distributing payments for the use of extracted bioinformation. Models for 'benefit sharing' do exist; they were first developed to distribute profits that arose from the exploitation of collected plant and animal genetic resources in the 1980s. It might seem, then, that such models could be mapped over to the human domain with relative ease. This does not prove to be the case. Deciding who could or should constitute a beneficiary is hugely complicated by the fact that human bioinformation (particularly genetic data) is a collective or familial resource that is shared and, thus, technically 'owned', by many. The political sensitivities that attend the collection and use of such resources have been particularly evident in cases where bioinformation has been extracted from marginalized indigenous communities. The fact that valuable samples and data were expropriated to the metropolitan centres of the West for use in pharmaceutical development without any reciprocal benefits being returned to the source communities raised considerable ire and led to charges that such collection practices were simply a new form of 'biocolonialism'.

An additional case study, Myriad's patenting of mutations in the BRCA 1 and BRCA 2 genes associated with breast cancer, allows us to unpack another thorny issue: whether simply isolating genes constitutes an act of discovery or invention. This is a significant question, because, as we now know, being able to successfully argue that isolation is an inventive act allows the 'inventor', so described, to make exclusive claims to rights of property in that invention. A detailed examination of the history of this landmark case helps us to trace the impact that the exercise of these rights has had on the ability of women to access vital breast cancer diagnostic tests. The case is significant as it demonstrates the impact that legal judgments on rights to ownership of bioinformation can have in shaping the everyday experiences of health and disease of many women who have a predisposition to that disease. This is especially significant given that, in many cases, these women were the unwitting and unrecompensed donors of the very resource on which such tests are based.

In Chapter 4, we develop some of these arguments about ownership to explore how bioinformation is bought to market: how it is capitalized on and by whom. Although we might – as individuals – see our bioinformation as our property, we generally lack the skills and resources to exploit it effectively. We therefore rely on scientists, medical professionals, entrepreneurs and corporations to bring that information to the market in the form of usable products. This means that we can only benefit from our bioinformation by placing it – or allowing it to be placed – in the hands of others. As we reveal in this chapter, while some of these recipients will use that data for our direct benefit, others will exploit it in ways that offer little direct benefit to us as donors and may even do us harm.

To explicate these arguments, we begin by examining the different ways in which bioinformation may be 'put to use' as a commercial resource. These range from using bioinformation as the basis of individual genetic tests that can indicate one's predisposition to a particular inherited condition or genetic ancestry, to large-scale population-wide studies conducted using biobanks that search for evidence of associations between genes and diseases. We also touch on more controversial uses of bioinformation by healthcare providers, including the use of genetic data (specifically the presence or absence of certain genetic mutations) to ration or triage access to treatment or drugs. Two case studies serve to illustrate how this works in practice. The first relates to the use of bioinformation to prioritize access to the breast cancer drug Herceptin in the UK; the second illustrates how racial information was used to exclusively market BiDil, a new treatment for severe heart failure, to the African American population in the United States. These cases, we argue, raise concerns over the stigmatization of populations linked to higher disease risk, and the potential reorganization of drug research along racial lines. Targeting populations on the basis of a perceived genetic risk can, theoretically, improve the delivery of healthcare. It is also clear that such practices provide opportunities for pharmaceutical developers to better identify those who constitute the greatest potential market for a given drug. While this improves access to advanced treatments for some, it reduces it for others whose diseases are relatively rare and thus have relatively smaller potential markets. Related concerns emerge over the 'interoperability' of ever expanding forensic and other kinds of security databases, such as those containing the data from airport screening. As we illustrate here, bioinformation that is collected for seemingly innocuous purposes or in the wider public interest (such as public health surveillance) can be harnessed to the geopolitical goals of national security and more controversial projects of subject identification – of distinguishing 'us' from 'them'.

Putting bioinformation to work is big business, and the

use of bioinformation inevitably goes hand-in-hand with its commodification. This is seen in the rapidly developing markets for personal genetic testing, drug discovery, forensic databases, biodefence and pharmacogenomics. We examine how this privatization of bioinformation was supposed to be balanced by the sharing of the benefits of this exploitation, but suggest that in practice this has proved very difficult to achieve. Conflicts still surround the question of who should benefit from the exploitation of bioinformation and how. Would donors, for example, prefer individual 'feedback' – as offered by some of the private sector genetic testing companies like 23andMe – or are guarantees of affordable access to any treatments developed more important? Other advocates suggest that we should prioritize the sharing of benefits with health services provided in the donor's immediate community, an important return for more altruistically minded donors. Such matters prove particularly significant, we suggest, for marginalized and indigenous communities whose members, due to long histories of inequality and exploitation, often have the greatest health needs but remain least likely to benefit from the genetic research in which they participate.

In Chapter 5 we turn to examine the future of the global economy in bioinformatic data, which proves to be, curiously enough, both big and small in scale. A key goal has been the development of personalized medicine, the idea that in the future a patient's treatment can be specifically tailored to their genetic, genomic, social and environmental profile. Yet in order to do this, scientists first need to think big, using large-scale population databases of people's genetic, environmental and medical history to trace associations between genes, environment and disease. These large-scale datasets result from the convergence of a number of technologies, practices and capabilities, including government initiatives to digitize national medical records, the creation of huge databases of

clinical and genetic response information amassed by pharmaceutical companies in the course of clinical trials, and the
public's embrace of a host of new online forums, apps and
wearable devices that now allow them to directly upload their
own bioinformation to the cloud.

The insights that analysing data on this scale can offer have
the potential to radically reform healthcare delivery, ensuring
that patients receive more timely and accurate diagnoses and
more clinically effective treatments. They can be used to track
the emergence of infectious disease, as was seen in the 2014
Ebola outbreak. Yet they also pose significant ethical, regulatory and legal challenges. It is these challenges that we address
in this chapter, including how to regulate access to the huge
volumes of highly sensitive personalized data that can be, and
is being, circulated, traded and exchanged instantaneously
in a globally expansive electronic economy for biodata. We
also query whether big data can deliver on its promises. To
date, attempts to find links between genes and diseases have
proved frustratingly elusive, while efforts to deliver improved
healthcare drawing on big data have been hampered by a
lack of resource and concerns over data security and privacy.
Nevertheless, many remain faithful to the vision that big data
can be used to predict an individual's propensity to disease and
how they may respond to treatments. Much of this work is actually performed by inferring the probability that an individual
with a particular profile will react in a given way. In thinking
through what might be problematic about such approaches,
we draw attention to the risks associated with drawing conclusions about individuals using meta-analyses of big data alone.

We also consider how the big data revolution has radically collapsed many of the principles that have underpinned
the operation of the bioinformational economy to date.
These include the importance of maintaining a clear distinction between public and private modes of exploitation, the

centrality of informed consent and the inviolability of privacy rights in personal bioinformation. The massification, interoperability and convergence of multiple datasets, many of which we unknowingly contribute to (or at least glancingly consent to with the click of an onscreen button) allows database analysts to 'know you without really knowing you'. We find ourselves disaggregated into numerous snippets of bioinformation, shared across public and private sector platforms, entered into Facebook profiles, caught as glimpses on a CCTV camera, exchanged on credit card purchase slips or filed in a medical record only to be reassembled algorithmically as an object of data analysis. This has serious implications for real-time interventions into our everyday lives, as our algorithmically defined selves become actionable avatars – the basis for determining our access to insurance or particular drugs or treatments.

Despite its name, the 'big data' agenda remains far from all-inclusive. In closing, we reflect on what and who might be excluded by this fashionable project of amassing ever larger conglomerations of bioinformation. Who exactly is being captured in the statistically defined populations and associations that emerge from big data enterprises? What kinds of norms are being generated by the search for associations between bioinformation and an individual's identity, ancestry, health or behaviour? Which populations and individuals find themselves either marginalized from, or exoticized by, their inclusion and exclusion from big databases, and to what effect? We invite our readers to reflect on what they and their communities might have to gain, and to lose, by allowing their bioinformation to be exploited, and if, indeed, they have any say either way.

In concluding, we look, in Chapter 6, to our bioinformational future, to consider how and in what ways we might better manage this increasingly valuable resource. In contrast to the logics of privatization that shaped early efforts to patent and claim ownership over bioinformation, there is now a growing recognition that the full value of bioinformation can only be realized if it is shared among researchers, whether publicly or privately funded. If this is the case, we ask how we might create and govern a bioinformational commons. In this chapter, we explore a number of different approaches to sharing bioinformation. These range from initiatives that have emerged from within the scientific research community that favour the open-sourcing or sharewaring of bioinformation as a 'foundational resource' to which all should have equal access, to others that draw on custodial models of charitable trusteeship. One promising approach is found in the idea of a 'solidaristic' approach to biobanking. This presumes that curators will no longer be obliged to protect biobank participants from *all* harm, but rather to recruit participants on the understanding that they are willing to risk *some* harm for the benefit of others. Instead of informed consent, they propose a model of informed participation. Other more radical approaches include the 'free the data' initiative, which employs crowdsourcing to fund the creation of bioinformatic databases that would be effectively 'owned' by the donors. In contrast to the custodianship and solidarity approaches, this model is designed to democratize control of donated bioinformational resources, allowing donors, rather than collectors, to determine how their data is used, by whom and to what ends.

Despite these promising initiatives, there remains a risk that the scope and scale of data generation and analysis under the big data agenda will be such that the majority of bioinformation collected will elude even these attempts to develop more open, sharing approaches to data management. An alternative might be, we conclude, to treat bioinformation in the same way that we treat other valuable commercial resources. Instead of seeking to control or limit who accesses them, we should instead promote their wide circulation, but tax their use. This model was first conceptualized for the regulation of

plant and animal genetic resources in the early 2000s,[19] but
the principle initially failed because technology was insuffi-
ciently advanced to make the tracing of bioinformational data
viable. This may, however, be about to change. If so, we could
be on the brink of a new political economy in which we begin
to ensure that at least some of the benefits of bioinformation
are returned fairly and equitably to those individuals and communities that provide one of the most extraordinarily valuable
raw materials of the twenty-first century.

Conclusion

Bioinformation is a term that has acquired considerable cur-
rency since the molecular revolution began to gain ground in
the mid-twentieth century. Despite becoming an extremely
value commodity for scientific and medical researchers, com-
paratively little is yet understood about how it is acquired,
used or commercialized. In this chapter, we have investigated
how bioinformation is extracted from tissues donated (either
voluntarily or unwillingly) by individuals to a range of publicly
and privately owned biobanks and anatomical collections. We
have pointed to some of the complexities that attend the collection and use of this curious resource – one that can exist in
a number of different registers simultaneously (as body part,
text, digital or electronic record). In the following chapters, we
chart the journeys that bioinformation makes as it proceeds
up and out of the human body, tracing its transformation
into a commodity of great interest and value to the global
pharmaceutical, diagnostic, forensic and medical research
communities. Along the way, we seek answers to the complex
moral and ethical questions that the commercialization of bioinformation has engendered. We begin by turning to the vital
question of where bioinformation comes from.

CHAPTER TWO

Provenance: Where Does Bioinformation Come From?

Introduction

A string of numerical code on a computer database appears at first glance to be about as far removed from a human being, with all their hopes, fears, dreams and relationships, as it is possible to be. Nevertheless, the sequence databases of the most significant genomic projects of the contemporary age are, of course, sourced from particular individuals and communities. Furthermore, the connections between bioinformation and its source populations, communities and individuals are what makes this data interesting and valuable. Unless we are able to trace the relationships between a piece of bioinformation (such as the presence or absence of particular genetic variants) and its phenotype (its impact on the health experiences of individuals in terms of their propensity to disease, disability, life expectancy and so on), then it can be largely meaningless. It is the ability to connect, for example, a shared inherited defect in a single gene to the likelihood of getting Huntingdon's disease that makes it a useful resource for biomedical research and treatment. The study of how genes are expressed or read by cells to produce particular phenotypes or health outcomes is known as epigenetics, and can be influenced by age, environment, lifestyle and disease. Accessing not only DNA or tissue samples, but also reliable and comprehensive associated contextual data is a key challenge for those seeking to collect, collate and exploit bioinformation. Other uses of bioinformation, such as those seen in forensic science, are also dependent on being able to map connections between DNA and specific individuals, family groups or suspect populations.

Consequently, biobanks or collections of bioinformation contain not only DNA, but also additional data about the individuals and communities that donate to them. Participating in a biobank requires individuals and communities to bequeath or sell more than just a sample of their DNA. They are often also asked to provide detailed information about family and life histories, or give permission for biobanks to access their medical records, or even to take part in extra medical examinations. In the future, the range of data that biobanks might seek may expand even further to include other sources of information, such as prescription histories or data from health apps on mobile phones or other devices, which would allow researchers to build an increasingly detailed picture of the 'environment' where genes are expressed, as we explore further in Chapters 5 and 6.

In this chapter, we ask who gives their bioinformation to such projects and why. Do they do so voluntarily? We consider whether those accessing an individual's bioinformation always need to ask for permission to create a biobank or to use biobanked data for a specific purpose or research project, and, if so, how that permission is obtained. We draw on the idea of 'provenance' to consider where bioinformation comes from, and how knowledge of its history shapes its perceived value and usefulness, as well as the impact that being seen as the source of particular kinds of bioinformation may have on donors. Provenance literally means origin or source, but is often used more specifically to refer to the history and ownership of an object that can later guide judgements of that object's authenticity or quality. The term is useful in pointing out the significance of knowing the history of a bioinformatic sample, who it came from and how it was obtained; attributes that similarly order its usefulness and value to research. It also suggests how, once detached from its source, bioinformation can become viewed and classified as an alienable 'object'. In this way 'provenance' captures both concerns with the source of bioinformation and how that sourcing shapes the way bioinformation is perceived and valued.

Where Does Bioinformation Come From?

French philosopher Michel Foucault argues that bioinformation – in the form of statistics about population health – was first systematically collected as a resource for public health purposes in the eighteenth century.[1] Collecting data about birth rates and causes of death offered officials, physicians and philanthropists the opportunity to map and understand incidences of health and disease at a national and later global scale. Physicians such as John Snow[2] and academics such as Edwin Chadwick[3] used bioinformation to inform public health interventions, such as improved sewerage systems and measures to reduce rubbish and pollution. However, long before this, bioinformation was also collected as part of the records of healthcare institutions (such as hospitals and asylums) by medical practitioners and by medical researchers and academics. Such information often formed part of the private collections of individual scientists and physicians, for whom their patients also constituted a key source of medical knowledge. This history offers an important context for understanding the contemporary collection and exploitation of bioinformation as both a public sector resource, utilized for the common good and promotion of public health, and as a resource for public and private sector medical research that many medical professionals and scientific researchers see as a product of their labour and therefore as belonging to them. Contemporary bioinformation is generated in much the same way as historical data, either purposefully collected by scientific researchers and public health practitioners as part of specific research projects, or amassed within public and private sector healthcare institutions during the process of providing patient care. Bioinformation has also been collected forensically (as Henry Elliot's case confirms: see Chapter 1) since the late nineteenth century. In the first section of this chapter, we explore the creation and later repurposing of biobanks as a resource for scientific and medical research and forensic science and the new private sector initiatives that allow the storage and interpretation of existing collections of bioinformation by individual consumers for the purposes of genealogical research and personal/family healthcare.

Building Biobanks for Medical and Scientific Research

If you want to build a biobank, there are two routes you might take. You might decide to establish a biobank from scratch, targeting a specific disease, patient group or community of interest. For example, UK Biobank,[4] established in 2007, is a purpose-built national health resource that has collected bioinformation – including blood, urine and saliva samples, physical measurements and detailed information about individual's lifestyles and medical history – from 500,000 volunteers aged 40–69 recruited between 2006 and 2010. UK Biobank is just one example of a range of biobanking projects. Recent decades have seen an explosion in the growth (and occasional failure) of newly created biobanks. Within Europe, national database projects include Iceland's HSD, Uman Genomics and the Karolinska Institutet-Biobank in Sweden, the Nord-Trøndelag health study (HUNT) in Norway, GenomEUtwin in Finland, and the Estonian Genome Project (EGP). In addition, there are international projects, such as the European Prospective Investigation into Cancer and Nutrition (EPIC,) which has recruited more than half a million participants across ten European countries. Outside Europe, there is the Singapore Tissue Network, the Public Population Project in Genomics (P3G) in Canada and the Chinese Kadoorie Study of Chronic Disease, among others. In addition to these, other kinds of biobanks are now emerging that focus on collecting and sequencing data that is not human DNA. For example, the US National Institute of Health's (NIH) Human Microbiome Project (HMP) collects data on the microbes found inside the human gut.

Despite broad similarities, each biobank has unique characteristics that reflect the provenance of the data they contain. First, they can vary in size, from relatively small collections focused on a particular disease or community, such as the 50,000 volunteers whose data is found in the Generation Scotland Bank, to deCODE Genetics' population database of around 100,000 Icelanders, to those such as UK Biobank and EPIC's target populations, which extend to a million or more participants. Second, funding and governance mechanisms also differ: the banks may be run as commercial enterprises (deCODE Genetics), public–private partnerships (UmanGenomics) or publicly funded charitable trusts (UK Biobank). Commercial funding of biobanking is becoming more commonplace but may raise particular concerns, especially if public resources are used to support such enterprises or when public and private interests come into conflict. For example, deCODE Genetics caused controversy when the Icelandic government created new legislation – the 1998 Act on a Health Sector Database – which allowed deCODE to access public medical record data for use in private sector research,[5] while UmanGenomics was created specifically to make banks of blood samples and health data developed by Umeå University and the local council of Västerbotten in Sweden available commercially, much to the consternation of some donors.[6]

Repurposing Existing Collections

A second way in which you might seek to build a biobank is by repurposing bioinformation originally collected for another purpose. Many hospitals, universities and commercial organizations, such as pharmaceutical companies, have collections of tissue and other sources of DNA material and related contextual data that effectively constitute inadvertent biobanks. For example, Guthrie cards[7] are a product of newborn screening programmes common in many countries across the developed world, including the United Kingdom, Australia and the United States. The midwife uses blotting paper card to collect small blots of blood from a heel prick. The name of the child or parent's name and the date of birth are recorded alongside the blood spots, enabling the blood sample to be linked to the child's medical records. The blood spots are screened for common, serious diseases that need to be treated rapidly after birth, including phenylketonuria (PKU), hypothyroidism and, more recently, cystic fibrosis (CF). Newborn screening can form the basis for earlier medical interventions, thereby preventing the onset of intellectual disabilities, serious illnesses or death. As a result, newborn screening programmes are an accepted 'standard of care' in many developed countries today.

Clinicians, health workers and parents generally agree that the newborn screening programme plays an important role in the early detection and treatment of treatable disorders. When it comes to the question of what exactly should be done with the cards once the initial screening process is complete, there is much less consensus. One argument for storing the cards for two years or more is the need to keep them for quality assurance purposes. Cards should be stored in order to allow for re-tests in case of inconclusive or false test results. In the United States, however, cards may be stored for much longer periods of up to 25 years, which inadvertently creates a database of DNA material with linked medical data. The fact that Guthrie cards contain both genetic material and personal data means scientists can identify which DNA profiles belong to individuals with particular medical conditions. This makes Guthrie cards a particularly desirable resource for research purposes.[8] For example, an Australian study used dried blood samples from Guthrie cards to try and establish if there was a relationship between CF and a predisposition to intussusception, a bowel condition.[9] Although the results of the study were negative, it did raise some interesting ethical questions about the repurposing of bioinformation collected in this way.

As with most medical research studies, the Australian team needed to seek scientific and ethical approval. Most countries have guidelines or procedures through which researchers can apply to use Guthrie card data in order to conduct genetic research, usually with the proviso that all personal identifying information be removed from the card. Recent indications suggest a growing public awareness of the values and risks associated with accessing such genetic data collections.[10] Permission may consequently be harder to gain and only offered under strict terms and conditions that specify exactly how the sample can be used. This is important, as Guthrie cards are also now being used for forensic purposes. In Australia, Guthrie card data has been used to identify relatives (and thereby potential victims) of the 2009 Victorian bushfires disaster,[11] and has even been seized by police for use in an incest prosecution.[12] Incidents like these have caused the public to question the retention of Guthrie cards and, in some cases (such as the incest case), led to calls for their destruction.

This kind of repurposing can also occur when biobanks themselves seek access to existing data about an individual participant. For example, UK Biobank asks patients for permission to access their existing and future medical records as well as collecting DNA samples. This can be controversial, especially when bioinformation moves from the public to the private sector. In 1998, the Icelandic government sparked an international debate and controversy when they passed the Act on a Health Sector Database (1998/139). The Act allowed the Icelandic Parliament to license a private company (deCODE Genetics) to create a centralized database using national medical records for use in gene discovery research. The repurposed medical record data would form one element of deCODE's biobank, and would be combined with information on family history (obtained through collaboration with Iceland-based company Frisk software) and DNA voluntarily donated by Icelanders to deCODE's collection. DeCODE then planned, in addition to using this resource for its own research, to make the database commercially available to customers who would pay to search the biobank for links between genes and diseases. DeCODE was particularly criticized (as we shall explore below) for its plans to use presumed consent (i.e., to assume that Icelanders were content for their medical record data to be repurposed in this way), instead of seeking the explicit informed consent of each and every Icelander.[13]

As a consequence of this and other objections (linked mainly to the commercial orientation of the proposed biobank), the Icelandic Act on a Health Sector Database met with significant opposition both locally and within the international community. Similarly, UmanGeonmics was created with the explicit objective of utilizing Sweden's existing blood bank for genetic research, but, following public outcry over the commercialization of public data, the company was brought under public oversight to assure the Swedish public the database would be used in the interests of the national community.[14] While the distinction between public and privately held databases was relatively secure in the late 1980s, it has since been progressively eroded as more bioinformation is routinely trafficked between each, a practice that makes the task of tracing where collected bioinformation goes and how it is used even more complex than it once was.

Forensic Biobanks

Arguably even more controversial than the national biobanks created for biomedical research are those databases established for forensic purposes. Forensic collections are usually established and stored separately from those used in medical practice and scientific and medical research, although historically there have been many cases where data has moved between the two – for example, the use of dental records in identifying victims of crime. Fingerprints were the earliest form of bioinformation to be systematically collected for forensic purposes and, as we explored in Chapter 1, the first fingerprint database was created in 1891. National DNA forensic databases are more recent, with the United Kingdom establishing the first one in 1995.[15] Today, according to the international policing agency Interpol, 120 countries use DNA profiling in criminal investigations, 54 countries have national DNA databases and a further 26 have plans to introduce a national DNA database, with Europe, North Africa and the Middle East having the highest levels of participation.[16] Recent years have also seen an increase in data sharing across national borders. For example, Interpol has an international database of more than 233,000 fingerprint records and more than 8,400 crime scene marks (as of October 2015).[17]

Personal Biobanking

Finally, there has been a growth in private sector biobanking, whereby individuals choose to 'bank' their bioinformation or send it for analysis to a private sector provider, either as a way of finding out more about their own ancestry or health (a kind of do-it-yourself personalized medicine) or as a form of insurance against future ill-health. The first of these is more common, with a range of commercial firms offering to sequence your DNA, each providing different forms of interpretive data 'packages'. One of the most well known of these companies is California-based 23andMe, which, for the sum of £125 (sterling) will send you a sampling kit. As the customer, you then provide a sample of your saliva and send it back to the company for sequencing. Once your DNA sample has been sequenced, the company interprets your data and suggests how your specific genetic traits may shape your health, including your potential predispositions to certain diseases and inherited conditions, and offers an estimate of what percentage of your DNA is Asian, European, sub-Saharan African, etc. However, as we shall see in Chapter 4, there are a number of concerns about the impact this information might have on you, the donor-customer, both psychologically and in terms of your health behaviour.

A more unusual but growing trend is for individuals to bank their own genetic material or that of their offspring by donating to cord blood banks. For some time now, individuals have been banking biological material in the form of gametes (human eggs and sperm) in order to maximize their chances of having children due to concerns over age or the impact of specific medical procedures (e.g., chemotherapy). Cord blood banks are different. Companies such as the Virgin Health Bank[18] in the United Kingdom offer new parents the opportunity to bank umbilical cord blood following the birth of their baby. Umbilical cord blood is a rich source of stem cells, which can be used to treat a range of medical conditions, including blood cancers. They also provide material for genetic sequencing and diagnosis, and it is envisioned they will be an increasingly important resource for biomedical research as well as health treatments in the future.

The methods used to assemble bioinformation have important implications for its provenance as they establish both where the data was sourced and also the history and life experiences of those who donated it. However, as we noted in the introduction, provenance also encompasses issues of data quality and authenticity. In the case of bioinformation, quality and authenticity are in turn shaped by the following key questions: (1) What motivates people to donate to biobanks (if they do so voluntarily)? (2) What protections and permissions are sought and needed to create and use bioinformation collections? (3) How does provenance affect data quality and how can this in turn lead to the characterization and in some cases stigmatization of source communities? These three issues are addressed in the remainder of this chapter. Provenance also has implications for questions of ownership, which we will explore further in Chapter 3.

Why Donate?

In the case of newly created biobanks, one of the key questions that emerges is why people would choose to participate. A recent poll conducted by the Progress Educational Trust[19] found a mixture of motivations, including the perceived importance of the research that would draw on the database, altruism, curiosity (from donor interested in their genetic make-up) and personal concerns about existing health conditions affecting the donor or their children. Some biobanks are even generated specifically to research a disease affecting a particular community. For example, in the 1990s the Native American Havasupai tribe consented to the collection of DNA samples as part of research into diabetes requested by the community. Often participants combine one or more of these motivations, suggesting that people's reasons for donating bioinformation are often complex and multiple. In contrast, those who collect bioinformation often expect people to donate voluntarily, anonymously and altruistically, without any expectation of direct benefits either to them or to their immediate family. For ethicist Ruth Chadwick, this raises a key issue in relation to biobanking, namely: what exactly is understood by the term 'benefit' and how is this perceived by biobank managers, users and donors?[20]

Historically, distinctions have been drawn between 'public' benefits, such as improvements to public health and medical care, and 'private' benefits, such as the commercial profits that private sector companies make from charging for access to bioinformation or from using it to develop pharmaceutical or diagnostic products. In the case of deCODE Genetics' proposed HSD, public benefits included a newly centralized computer medical records database, an annual licence fee of 70 million Icelandic krona (US$1 million), a share in the profits of any drugs developed and the potential benefits of future research into the prevention, diagnosis and treatment of disease. 'Private' benefits included the profits the company made from selling access to the database. Other benefits are less easy to characterize as either strictly public or private: the prestige, wealth and jobs that Iceland secured from having a large and successful genomics firm is a good example. While the professionals involved in the creation of biobanks are convinced that donors participate with no expectation of receiving direct benefits, participants seem less sure of this. In a 2007 public meeting in Oxford about UK Biobank, one of the participants asked what would happen if UK Biobank's research produced information pertinent to their healthcare as an individual. Would that information be fed back to them or their doctor?[21] As Helen Busby notes in her study of participants donating blood to the UK national blood service, donors' motives are not always purely altruistic; they also see themselves as donating to a bank that they and their relatives could later draw on. Other elderly donors explained that donating also functioned as a kind of 'health check'.[22]

Patients are not, however, usually given details of the results of research undertaken using information donated to a genetic database, even if they relate directly to their care, although the question of whether feedback should be provided to biobank donors is now being actively discussed in the academic literature.[23] Medical experts are concerned that most research data has little clinical significance for individual patients and that donors lack the expertise to make sense of research findings, a matter we explore further in Chapter 4. Conversely, it could be argued that patients have a right to be made aware of (or indeed to not know[24]) any research outcomes that may have implications for their health, research findings that could be discussed with them by their doctor. Some even suggest that biobank operators and researchers could potentially be held legally liable for any failure to warn donors about findings derived using their bioinformation that have significant implications for their health. One exception to the general trend of no feedback from genetic databases is the EGP, in which participants were promised the right to access information to inform their own healthcare. Interestingly, a survey found this was a major incentive for people intending to donate their samples to the databank.[25]

Other voices have questioned whether people should benefit financially from their participation in genetic biobanks, particularly those run commercially by the private sector. In Iceland, a group of lawyers caused a furore in February 2000 when they contacted prospective donors and suggested they should opt out of the Icelandic HSD in order to sell their records back to deCODE at a later date. This proposal was strongly criticized as unethical by the Icelandic ministry of health, which categorically stated that deCODE was not permitted to pay individuals in return for their participation in the database.[26] The message here seemed to be that not only should individuals not directly benefit from participation in a biobank, but that to do so would be ethically inappropriate. Here we see a significant difference emerging in the way bioinformation is perceived and valued: what kind of object it is thought to be, and who might be considered its rightful owner. In this Icelandic example, bioinformation was positioned as a national resource to be managed and exploited by the state, rather than being viewed as the private property of the individuals from whom it was derived.

We might also ask the question, 'why not donate?'. Well, participation in genetic databases also carries some risks, and an onus is placed on both ethics review committees (which review applications to create and use biobanks) and individual donors to weigh up the risks against the benefits of participation. We have already spent some time exploring the potential benefits of donating bioinformation to a biobank, but what are the risks? Physical risks are small, but participation does involve other social risks, notably around data privacy. No matter how well the data is protected or anonymized there is always the possibility that the information may be circulated to others without the donor's consent. Individuals or companies may illegally access the data, or it may be requisitioned by court order. In addition, while an individual may not be identified, there is the risk of being associated with the findings of the study. While this association can bring prestige, if the findings were, for example, to link the study population to a particular disease, there is a risk that all members of that population will be exposed to stigmatization and discrimination. We will return to discuss the implications of this in the following chapters. Concerns about the risks of participating in biobanks and participants' motivations for doing so have implications for both the way in which permission is sought (or not) from donors and for the measures taken to protect donor identity and privacy, and it is to these questions that we now turn.

Data Protection and Anonymity

As we have noted above, for bioinformation to be valuable for research purposes, it needs to be linked to some degree to a set of information about the health status of the individual(s) or population(s) from whom that data is derived, and its value can often increase as more information about that/those individual(s)' health, physiology and environment is added. This, in and of itself, may be a source of controversy, as medical and bioinformation are commonly viewed across many societies as comprising some of the most personal and private information there is. Given what bioinformation might be able to reveal about individuals, their family or their community, confidentiality and data protection are often key issues for those who create and manage bioinformatic resources and those who participate in them. People are particularly concerned that insurance companies may seek, and be granted, access to identifiable genetic information, and that this may be used to discriminate against individuals whose medical data shows they are at risk of inheriting certain medical conditions. Biobanks consequently need to comply with national data protection legislation and protect the identities of their participants.

For these reasons, researchers may seek to completely anonymize collected bioinformation. Theoretically, this is the most secure way of storing data, as the individual who supplied the information can no longer be identified other than through DNA testing. However, many biobanks wish to retain the ability to link participants and their bioinformatics record. One reason for this may be to add further data either to enrich the record as more information (e.g., from lifestyle apps) becomes available, or to reflect changes in an individual's health that might be very pertinent to understanding links between genes and diseases. Another reason may be the need to trace donors to inform them about findings of direct relevance to their health. For example, the Australian Guthrie card study cited above sparked a debate about the use of one-way encryption.[27] Scientists, it was argued, were left in a 'strange (and unethical) position' when research they conducted on the cards identified donors who were carrying the CF gene but who could not be told as the anonymization was irreversible. The case provoked a range of responses: some suggested that data should be identifiable, others that a wider array of disorders should be screened for in the first place.[28] These concerns point to the question of who should benefit from the exploitation of bioinformation and how, a matter we return to in Chapter 4.

Issues of data privacy can, in theory, be overcome in healthcare research by using anonymized, or at least non-personally identifiable bioinformation. Biodata of interest to researchers that comes with a provenance can be effectively 'washed' so that key information on age, health history and medical referrals is retained, while data that could be used to trace the bioinformation back to the individual (name, address, etc.) is removed from the bioinformatic database. Many bioinformation resource managers will go to considerable lengths to try and guarantee participant privacy by creating coded samples.[29] This refers to samples that are given a unique identifier (distinct from other easily recognized codes such as birth date), so that, although the identity of the person is concealed, the samples can be traced and the dataset updated with, say, details of changes to the individual's health. However, this process also poses challenges. Some of the information that could be very revealing about the social and environmental factors which shape gene expression and disease outcomes, for example an individual's place of residence or work, can also be identifying information.

To limit such risks, statistical methods can be employed to restrict the ways in which it is possible to access and query the bioinformation database so that it becomes very difficult to trace data back to individuals. For example, those who consult or query bioinformation databases may only be able to recall information about groups of people, as opposed to individuals, or to secure statistical averages rather than precise data about age. Despite all this, many companies have now devised complex algorithmic software that enables researchers to pool and cross-reference bioinformation from several different bioinformational databases at once – including, for example, credit card databases, genetic sequence databases and electronic health record databases (something we will return to in Chapters 5 and 6). This allows them to 'triangulate' searches in ways that make it possible to identify individuals from a combination of anonymized and identifiable records. The implications of this for data privacy are extremely serious, to say the least.

Ethics and Informed Consent

One of the key objections raised in the Guthrie card case was that parental consent wasn't sought for the repurposing of their children's bioinformation. The question of when and how those who generate and exploit bioinformatics databases should secure specific informed consent is a key bioethical issue. Since the Second World War, when Nazi researchers carried out experiments on unwilling prisoners of war who were suffering obvious harm, informed consent has been a leading principle in the conduct of medical research, formalized in the Nuremberg Code of 1946 and in the Helsinki Declaration of 1964:

In any research on human beings, each potential subject must be adequately informed of the aims, methods, sources of funding, any possible conflicts of interest, institutional affiliations of the researcher, the anticipated benefits and potential risks of the study and the discomfort it may entail. The subject should be informed of the right to abstain from participation in the study or to withdraw consent to participate at any time without reprisal. After ensuring that the subject has understood the information, the physician should then obtain the subject's freely-given informed consent, preferably in writing. If the consent cannot be obtained in writing, the non-written consent must be formally documented and witnessed.[30]

Viewed as essential for any research project or clinical trial using human volunteers, the extent to which this principle applies to participants in biobanks remains a controversial issue within both academic and professional communities. Some suggest it is rapidly becoming obsolete in the face of the growing interoperability of databases, while others insist that the public should be informed of the studies that are being conducted on their medical data. Others argue such a process would be unfeasible: gaining consent from each individual patient for every new prospective study would be a bureaucratic nightmare that would dramatically slow the pace of vital health research. There is no one answer.[31] What the diversity of responses points to are the ethical difficulties presented by resources like Guthrie cards, which cross the boundaries between medicine and scientific research, personal and public interests.

The repurposing of medical records was also a key source of controversy in the creation of the deCODE Genetics Bank in Iceland. Rather than seeking the individual consent of each Icelander whose medical records were to be included in the database, deCODE instead approached the Icelandic government with a proposal for a new piece of legislation (which was later to become the 1998 Icelandic Act on a Health Sector Database) that would effectively license a private company (such as deCODE) to create a centralized database of anonymized Icelandic medical records for use in biomedical research. Objection to this scheme was immediate and vociferous. Those who protested, including both international academics and a local opposition group, Mannvernd (the Association of Icelanders for Ethics in Science and Medicine), raised a number of concerns, and in particular two key issues stood out. First, protesters strongly objected to the use of 'presumed' consent. Icelanders were not asked if they wanted to participate; it was simply presumed that they would not object to their medical records being used in such ways. Of course, in reality, many did object, and the legislation was later amended to afford them an opportunity to opt-out of having their information included if they so wished. A second concern was the fact that deCODE was effectively exploiting a public sector resource for private profit. For some, this goes against the altruistic social contract that arguably underpins many donors' desire to participate in biobanks – namely, the assumption that publicly held biomedical data is a commonly held resource and should be exploited only in the broad common interest.

Having learnt from the controversy surrounding deCODE's Health Sector Database, most newly created biobanks now seek participants' explicit consent. Volunteers arriving to donate to UK Biobank undergo a specific informed consent protocol. However, the unique characteristics of bioinformation poses problems for the process of gaining informed consent from biobank donors. Informed consent is usually defined as the freely given consent of an individual who has been given sufficient information to assess the risks and benefits of participation, but these risks and benefits are difficult to anticipate in the case of a biobank since the possible future uses of the data it holds remain to be determined. Furthermore, genetic information does not just refer to an individual; it also contains information about their family, but informed consent makes no provision for the different family members to inform the decision to participate or not.

Those responsible for biobanks therefore find themselves trying to balance out the needs both of researchers, who require access to the resource for as long as possible as well as the scope to put that resource to a wide variety of uses, and of donors, many of whom argue that they expect to have a say in how their data is used. Some, however, question whether donors have the expertise, autonomy or willingness to make a truly informed decision. Informed consent places responsibility on the patient to weigh up risks and benefits of participation, which will require donors to actively engage with and digest complex bodies of information on all future studies and projects that may employ their data.[32] Numerous authors have already noted the lack of engagement and interest displayed by research participants in existing consent forms. Most are happy to let others make decisions for them, and critics suggest that the fact that donors are asked to consent to participate by medical or scientific personnel in a clinical setting can serve to make consent feel more compulsory than voluntary.[33]

Slightly different concerns arise when it comes to forensic bioinformation. In many countries, rather than being donated, forensic bioinformation can be taken forcibly from suspect populations and individuals in the interests of detecting and preventing crime. Forensic bioinformation may also be collected from those who have witnessed crimes, but this usually requires their informed consent. According to a recent report by the Nuffield Council on Bioethics,[34] the United Kingdom has, per head of population, one of the largest forensic DNA databases in the world, accounting for around

4 million samples or 6 per cent of the population. This is in part due to a series of Acts of Parliament that have expanded police powers to forcibly take and retain biological samples from suspects in cases where a recordable crime has been committed. In England and Wales (in contrast to much of the rest of Europe) it was permissible for samples collected before 2012 to be held indefinitely, even if the arrestee was never actually convicted. The indefinite retention of samples from those who were not convicted, from witnesses who volunteered their samples, and from minors (those under 18 years of age), in a criminal database, was seen as an example of what is termed 'mission creep': when the remit of a database expands without attention or regulation, allowing more and more individuals to be accessioned without appropriate justification. A later judgment from the European Court of Human Rights determined that this progressive expansion was a step too far, and ruled that all samples from volunteers, minors and those not convicted should be removed from the police DNA databases for all but the most serious crimes.

Provenance and Bioinformatic 'Quality'

The issue of consent is important because it forms one aspect of the perceived 'quality' of bioinformation. Indeed, Emma Kowal suggests the ethical provenance of biobanked information is as important to its value as the contextual and health experience data of the individual from whom the data is acquired.[35] Collections of bioinformation that are controversial or that have been gathered or prepared in ways that are seen as unethical are much less attractive for end users as they may raise problems further down the line, notwithstanding any personal qualms users may feel about accessing such data. For example, publication in peer-reviewed academic journals is key to the status and credibility of many leading researchers, but journals may refuse to publish research where the data has not been collected in accordance with agreed ethical norms. Conversely, bioinformation collected by organizations or biobanks with high ethical standards, and which are viewed as having have good relationships with their participants, is seen as more desirable.[36] The relationship between bioinformatic donors and bioinformation users thus plays a vital role in establishing and authenticating the provenance of bioinformation.

Kowal has also written about these issues in the Australian context, noting how the thousands of blood samples taken from Australia's indigenous peoples held in collections across the global North are becoming more ethically complex as standards and accepted practice in genetic sample collections change. Increasingly, the use of these samples has come under fire, and a requirement has been added that indigenous communities have a guardian or spokesperson who grants permission for their use. Ensuring their status as 'ethically collected and used' samples is particularly significant for indigenous populations who have been marginalized politically, culturally and socially through long colonial histories of exploitation and oppression that have adversely impacted their health and quality of life. Without this added dimension of provenance – what Kowal calls added 'ethical biovalue' – these resources become 'orphan DNA', without sufficient attribution to be used ethically.

Other aspects of provenance may also affect the perceived 'quality' of the data. These can include the nature and characteristics of the population from whom the data is obtained. Biobank operators draw on attributes of their source populations to market the quality and usefulness of the resources they are creating. For example, in scoping out the possibility of creating the Icelandic HSD, Kevin Kinsella, then Chief Executive Officer of US-based genetics firm Sequana, highlighted the presence of 'founder effects', unique genetic variants found in perhaps one or two original settlers, which, over time, become amplified in this relatively isolated population, creating a distinctive set of inherited genetic variations and traits.[37] Other indigenous populations (such as Australian aboriginals) are similarly valued, as their long isolation is thought to create the potential for the development of novel genetic variations. In contrast, for UK Biobank the *heterogeneity* of the UK population is a key selling point, offering scope to explore a wide range of genetic variants and associated medical conditions. Other biobanks focus on particular medical conditions: For example, the 100,000 Genomes Project specifically targets participants with cancer and rare diseases and their blood relatives. These examples highlight how the use and collection of DNA is inseparable from the ways that use and collection is rationalized. This inevitably has implications for how source populations are imagined and characterized, respectively, as (1) 'inbred', genetically distinct and isolated, (2) heterogeneous and ethnically diverse, or (3) at increased risk of developing rare diseases.

These 'marketing' strategies are important socially and culturally because they signal the ways in which participating in a biobank can impact not just an individual but their entire community. As noted above, to participate in a biobank, particularly one targeting a particular disease or condition, is to run the risk of being associated with that condition, and the potential stigma and discrimination (including the familiar spectre of discrimination by health and life insurance providers) that may result from that association. Although there are also many positive associations that may arise from altruistically participating in a biobank project, one key case that highlights some of the more negative effects is the Human Genome Diversity Project's collection, analysis and controversial catergorization of genetic samples and information from many thousands of indigenous populations, which they describe as 'isolates of historic interest'.[38]

The aim of the HGDP, led by geneticist Luigi Luca Cavalli-Sforza, was to sample and capture global genetic diversity and use this data to model human migrations over the past 100,000 years.[39] The project is framed as being explicitly anti-racialist, based on the argument that, by seeking to find the common genetic legacies of humankind, it will undermine the idea that race is genetically determined and that different races are biologically distinct. Biological determinism has long raised concerns due to its close association with eugenics and arguments for the supremacy of white and Western ethnicities over other races, but, as Jenny Reardon and Kim TallBear argue, the way in which HGDP scientific data is collected – by Western scientists, for Western goals, and from marginalized native peoples – confounds the assumption that antiracialist research is always, by definition, antiracist.[40] Indeed, they suggest that the ways in which the data was collected and used by the HGDP echoed long histories of biocolonialism, whereby the human remains (especially skulls) of indigenous populations were collected and used by European colonists to support eugenic ideas – histories which geneticists often seem to know surprisingly little about.[41]

Emphasizing the anti-racialism of the HGDP also runs the risk of promoting only the benefits of genetic research for source communities through assertions that the genetic knowledge gained will provide further insights into the specific disease histories and experiences of indigenous populations. Missed is the way in which, as noted above, genetic knowledges about population and migration history may also be drawn on by the state to undermine indigenous claims to identity, territory and property: in short, to prove they are not indigenous enough. Such approaches also continue the tradition of assuming that Western science (seen in the creation and analysis of biobanks) provides the only, or at least the most definitive, way of making use of bioinformation, denying the possibility that indigenous peoples may have their own ways of making sense of this information and may wish to retain knowledge and control over their genomic data. We will go on to explore in more detail these questions of ownership and property rights in Chapter 3.

Conclusion

The aim of this chapter has been to consider bioinformatic provenance; questions about where bioinformation comes from and how this affects the ways it is perceived and valued. We began by outlining some of the key ways in which bioinformation is collected to construct entirely new biobanks and forensic databases, or repurposed from existing collections so it can be made available anew for further research and analysis. We then explored different individuals' motivations to donate to biobanking projects or to allow their bioinformation to be incorporated into such banks. We noted here that the altruistic motivations that many biobankers assume donors have are, in fact, often accompanied by more personal concerns and motivations, including expectations of direct feedback of data or other benefits. We noted how managing these expectations is a key concern for those seeking permission or consent to create a biobank. We also explored the difficulty of achieving a balance between protecting individual donors' privacy and anonymity and maintaining the links between bioinformation and its human provenance necessary both to permit feedback (if allowed) and strengthen medical and forensic research.

Finally, we examined how participation in biobanks can also reflect back onto source populations and communities. The ways in which particular source populations are characterized as 'homogenous', 'heterogenous' or 'isolates of historic interest' has implications for the ways in which both that data and its source population are viewed, and – particularly in the case of indigenous communities – risks repeating ethically questionable biocolonial practices and assumptions. Each of these cases demonstrates how the provenance of bioinformation is key to the way in which that information is valued. If bioinformation lacks provenance, it is impossible to link genetic information to human experiences of health and disease, or to the presence and absence of individuals at the scene of a crime. If bioinformation lacks provenance, ethical concerns and questions are raised about how that data was collected and whether it can be used ethically in research. As we shall go on to explore in Chapter 3, the provenance of bioinformation also has implications for who is seen as being the rightful owner of these increasingly valuable bioinformatics resources.

CHAPTER THREE

Property: Who Owns Bioinformation?

Introduction

The process of making bioinformation accessible, available and readable takes time, energy and money. Much of the bioinformation that exists in databases around the world today has been generated from DNA sequencing, often as part of larger scientific efforts to sequence whole genomes. The cost of whole genome sequencing is determined, in part, by the size of the genome, which varies by organism. *E. Coli* (a bacterium that lives in the gut) has a genome of 5 million base pairs and fruit flies a genome of 123 million base pairs. The most complex of all is the human genome, with approximately 3 billion base pairs. The task of sequencing it, which began in 1990 and concluded in 2003, was immensely complex, requiring scientific input from researchers working in public institutions and private corporations and consortia. The final cost of the enterprise is estimated to have been between US$500 million and US$1 billion. The story of how the sequence was generated is instructive because it provides some key insights into the questions that this chapter seeks to address: who owns bioinformation? How do they come to own it? And what does owning bioinformation make possible?

The Human Genome Project (HGP),[1] designed to enable the identification and mapping of all the nucleotides of the human genome, was initially promoted by the Reagan administration in the United States, which authorized and funded the Department of Energy and the NIH to coordinate plans for its development. These involved creating a genuinely international network of scientific institutes that each contributed to the sequencing endeavour.[2] One of the purposes of the project was to use the maps to chart and explain how genetic variations affect an individual's risk of developing certain diseases or conditions. Francis Collins, then director of the National Human Genome Research Institute, described its significance and utility for medical research by drawing on increasingly popular informational metaphors. In 2001, commenting on the completion of the first draft, he suggested that the genome could be thought of as 'a history book – a narrative of the journey of our species through time. It's also a shop manual, with an incredibly detailed blueprint for building every human cell ... and it's a transformative textbook of medicine, with insights that will give health care providers immense new powers to treat, prevent and cure disease.'[3] The work was undertaken by 20 publicly funded universities and institutions from across the globe to help determine the causes of and cures for some of most debilitating conditions that affect humankind as part of their wider 'service to society'.

Bioinformation of this type was clearly going to have very significant commercial, as well as purely scientific, value. For these reasons, a rivalrous operation was set up by the corporation Celera Genomics, headed by Craig Venter, who proposed to complete a draft of human genome ahead of the HGP for a mere US$300,000. How, though, could this possibly be achieved? Concerned that the HGP was becoming bogged down in political infighting, Venter determined to set up his own sequencing team which would accelerate production by using a rapid, automated technique described as 'shotgun sequencing', applying it to sequence information already generated by the HGP's publicly funded collaborating institutions. Celera proposed to use expressed sequence tags (unique sections of 150–400 base pairs) to identify the genes from which they came, and to then guess at the function of these genes by finding others of similar structure and known function through computerized searches of publicly available genomic databases. Although he initially declared that his sequences would be made freely accessible to the public, as were those of the HGP, Venter later determined to make key bioinformation available only to paying customers via subscription to Celera's genomic sequence databases. Further controversy erupted when Venter declared his intention to file for preliminary patents on more than 6,000 genes and full utility patents on a further 200–300 genes before releasing their sequences into the public domain. The privatization of bioinformation had clearly begun – but how had this become possible?

Owning Bioinformation

Scientists involved in the HGP were primarily rewarded for generating this vital resource via recognition and scientific attribution of their contributions to the project. Privately funded corporations such as Celera sought additional monetary returns on their financial investments. To do this, they needed to be able to charge users to access their genetic databases. This could only be achieved if they were able successfully to assert and defend claims of ownership to that bioinformation. This, initially, seemed unlikely. In 1996, scientific leaders had together agreed on a ground-breaking set of principles for the sharing of bioinformatic data (known as the Bermuda Agreement), which established that 'all DNA sequence data should be released into publicly accessible databases within twenty-four hours of generation'.[4] US President Bill Clinton thus declared on the eve of the publication of the final draft of the human genome that all human genetic material and information would remain 'unpatentable'. Despite this, many genes, sequences and mutations that confer increased risk of contracting diseases, such as breast cancer and Alzheimer's, have since been claimed as 'inventions' to which private rights of property may obtain. So too have other products manufactured from human tissue, such as cell lines and stem cells. But how can bodily material and information from human beings be characterized and defended in law as private property that can be bought and sold on the open market, especially when it is commonly understood that the ownership of human beings and body parts is prohibited?

One of the key invocations of moral philosopher Immanual Kant was to 'act so that you treat humanity whether in your own person, or in that of another, always as an end and never as a means only'.[5] In Kant's view a clear distinction can and should be drawn between those things that can be priced and those that should not be, such as human life. This conception forms the basis of what are termed dignitarian arguments against practices, processes or products that compromise human dignity, including the commodification of the human body. Since the Abolition of Slavery Act (1833) was introduced in the West, it has become an established societal norm that no legal system will allow one person to hold or exercise a private property right in respect of another person. As legal historian Robin Hickey puts it, 'ownership' of persons is, in this sense, a 'legal impossibility' in the modern world.[6] Yet, while ownership of whole persons is subject to legal prohibition, bodily parts can, and have, been bought and sold. Although immorally and illegally obtained, the organs and tissues extracted by notorious body snatchers of the eighteenth century, such as William Burke and William Hare, found their way into markets for anatomical specimens, while the contemporary organ trade sees kidneys and other bodily parts traded in black markets. These are not, however, transactions that are sanctioned either societally or in law. How, then, can body parts and the information that they contain enter a state of being legally recognized property and commodities?

When body parts or human tissues remain within the fabric of the body or are still identifiably part of it, they are usually perceived to be, as legal scholar Margaret Radin suggests, so 'bound up with the person as to be of unique and nonmonetizable value to that person'.[7] However, as we have seen, these tissues have utility in many kinds of biomedical research and in clinical practice. Making them available for this kind of use means that they must undergo processes of transformation. Human tissue is corruptible and will decompose if left in its natural state. To prevent this, it must first be stabilized, that is to say, rendered in a more technological or artefactual form. This can involve fixing the tissue and mounting it on glass slides, growing a population of cells from a single cell that can be kept alive in a laboratory, or even reading the informational content of a cell and notating that as a sequence or set of sequences stored on an electronic database.

Making Biotechnological Inventions

Manufacturing these kind of new renderings of human tissue is a complex and time consuming affair, one that requires specialist expertise. As the historian of science Hannah Landecker notes in her compelling history of the emergence of tissue culturing,[8] such technical triumphs take many years of concerted work to achieve, even if, once perfected, they can then be fairly easily mass-produced. What is termed the theory of natural law holds that property arises as a consequence of the assertion of labour on natural resources. If we consider that all of the Earth's natural resources form part of the common wealth of humanity, how can any one person justify claiming exclusive ownership of any part of it? An answer to this question was first offered by political philosopher John Locke, who asserted in his *Second Treatise of Government* that such a right of property could arise when individuals mix their labour (which they themselves own) with that which is unowned, generating in the process an object that would not otherwise have existed, and that they consequently have a right to claim as theirs. Such a theory rests on what James Tully calls 'the workmanship model': that makers have property rights in respect of the things they make.[9]

The application of this concept to the protection of new biotechnological inventions was first evidenced in the landmark case of *Diamond v. Chakrabarty*, determined in the US Supreme Court in 1980.[10] Chakrabarty, a scientist working for the General Electric corporation, had applied for an industrial patent on a bacterium that he had genetically engineered to break down crude oil spills. The application was initially rejected on the basis that microorganisms are 'products of nature' and, as such, unpatentable under Section 101 of the US Constitution. The aim of the founding fathers in making this exclusion was to ensure that individuals or industries were prevented from 'securing a monopoly on living organisms, no matter how produced or how used'.[11] The Supreme Court judges were later to decide in a very close 5–4 judgment that Chakrabarty should, in fact, be granted a patent on his bacterium on the grounds that it was first and foremost a 'manufacture'. Following the workmanship model, Chakrabarty was deemed to have 'invented' a novel microorganism by finding a way of successfully combining four plasmids and inserting them into one bacterium, thereby crafting from existing natural materials a non-naturally occurring entity. Patents, when granted, give inventors exclusive rights to dictate who may use their inventions and to levy royalties (charges) for their use, a monopoly that remains in place for between 17 and 20 years. This legal precedent was highly significant because it established the right to patent biotechnological inventions, including those based on human tissues, cells and extracted bioinformation.

Patenting Immortal Cell Lines

Among the first such patents to be granted was that awarded to the University of Southern California (USC) for a human cell line. In 1976, Mr John Moore, who was suffering from hairy-cell leukaemia, followed the recommendation of his physician, Dr David Golde of the UCLA Medical Center, and had his spleen removed in order to slow the progress of his disease. On examination, Golde discovered that Moore's spleen contained particularly unusual T-lymphocytes capable of producing two strains of white blood cells with heightened capacity to fight bacteria. Golde and his research associate Shirley Quan, who also worked at USC, recognized that these cells had great therapeutic value in limiting infections in both cancer and HIV patients. Cells extracted from an organism cannot usually reproduce themselves indefinitely outside the body. Those kept alive in culture medium will normally undergo only about 50 cycles of cell division before ceasing to proliferate. Working assiduously over the next three years, Golde and Quan developed a means of keeping the cells extracted from Mr Moore's spleen alive indefinitely in culture medium, creating what we now term an 'immortalized cell line'. In 1984, USC applied successfully for a patent (No. 4438032) on this biotechnological invention, which it christened the 'Mo Line'.

Golde and Quan, as named inventors, were then positioned to enter into exclusive contractual arrangements with two biotech firms, the Genetics Institute of Massachusetts and Sandoz Pharmaceuticals, to commercialize the line and any derivations of it. Although their clinical potential was not yet fully established, reports in biotechnology journals at the time predicted that the likely market value of these lymphokines would be approximately US$3 billion by 1990, and both inventors received hundreds of thousands of dollars in advance payments from the Genetics Institute and Sandoz for their contributions. When Moore, the original patient, became aware of these arrangements, he sued Dr Golde, claiming redress for breaching his professional obligations (in not informing Moore about his intended repurposing of the tissue or seeking his consent), and an ownership stake in the patented Mo cell line. The Supreme Court of California, while agreeing that Golde had failed in his duties to Moore by not informing him of his planned reuse of the excised tissue, nevertheless rejected Moore's claim to shared ownership of the line.

The legal justification for rejecting Moore's claim is interesting. The Court ruled that when individuals agree to surgery, they implicitly accept that the excised tissue will be discarded as waste after the procedure and thus cannot reasonably expect to retain an interest in its fate. As individuals are not considered in law to have any legal rights of ownership to their organs or tissues, Moore could not claim interference with an existing right of personal property. Perhaps most significantly, the Court upheld the judgment arrived at in the Chakrabarty case, namely, that the Mo cell line, although derived from Moore's tissue, was no longer simply a body part but had been so substantially modified by the application of Golde and Quan's skill and expertise as to have become a manufactured 'invention'. While Moore was viewed as having contributed the raw bodily material, it was Golde and Quan alone who were considered to have applied the intellectual labour necessary to make the bioinformation embodied in it available for use in this novel form. This explains why they, and not Moore, were named as inventors of the line and were thus granted exclusive rights to extract commercial value from its applied use.[12]

A similar controversy arose in relation to what is now perhaps the most widely used cell line in modern biotechnological research. The HeLa line is named after the African American cervical cancer patient Henrietta Lacks, from whom it was sourced in 1951. Lacks first attended Johns Hopkins University Hospital for intermenstrual bleeding, which proved to be a symptom of cervical cancer. Lacks unwittingly became part of a wider biomedical research project at the hospital when a biopsy of her tissue was sent to the laboratories of George and Margaret Gey without her knowledge or permission. This lack of consent was not unusual at this time and resulted from the prevailing view that discarded bodily material belonged not to the individual from whom it was sourced, but, rather, to the researcher or institution that had acquired possession of it. To the researchers' great surprise, Lacks' cancerous cells proved capable of doing what normal cells could not – they continued to grow, divide and rapidly proliferate in culture medium for indefinite periods of time. The unique genetic composition of her cells allowed them to become an extremely valuable research tool. As they were essentially clonal, they provided a 'standard example' of human cells and thus a means through which to perform comparative analyses of cell reaction to viruses, bacterial infections, toxicity, pharmaceuticals and other treatments.

As Gey's development of the line predated the concept that scientific objects or techniques could be viewed as biotechnological inventions, he never sought to patent HeLa, but instead distributed it free of charge to his research colleagues. Later, as the utility of the line became more apparent, biological supply companies began to grow and sell the HeLa line commercially, and it has since become the key underpinning resource of thousands of subsequently developed commercial products, patents and discoveries. In her 2010 book, *The Immortal Life of Henrietta Lacks*,[13] Rebecca Skloot highlights the bioethical questions raised by this case. One of these questions – namely, why it is that the family of the woman whose cells have been vital to the generation of a series of financially lucrative vaccines have been unable to share in the proceeds arising from their sale – will be addressed in more detail in Chapter 4. A second question, regarding the legitimacy of using tissue derived from medical procedures for commercial purposes, has also raised significant concerns for individuals and their families. Such matters become even more complex when the extracted material is drawn from wider populations that share particular genetic traits.

Population Wide Genetic Research

In 1991, the US NIH patented a cell line developed from the DNA of a Hagahai donor (US patent 5397696). The Hagahai are an indigenous group of people in Papua New Guinea whose isolated existence had led them to develop a concentration of particular genetic variants and mutations. Following appeals from the Hagahai for help in understanding a disease that was afflicting their community, researchers from the NIH found that the tribe carried a gene that predisposed them to leukaemia while leaving them symptom-free. This variant was later found to be human T-lymphotrophic virus (HTLV), which showed potential for use as a leukaemia vaccine, and a patent was granted on this HTLV-infected cell line. The patent provoked considerable controversy for a number of reasons. Although samples were only taken from a small number of the tribe members, the mutation is prevalent throughout the group. Some individuals gave a basic informed oral consent to participate in the research. However, as the resources that they were agreeing to donate (in this case, valuable genetic information) were not unique to them, they were also effectively providing de facto permission to participate from kin who had neither been consulted nor given their consent.[14]

While it has become evident that *individual* models of consent and property rights are insufficient in such situations, it is not yet clear what form a communal model of consent could ideally take. Groups, of course, can be variously constituted. They may consist of a 'collective' of individuals who share similar concerns and interests about the prospective ownership and use of their genetic information. Those individuals who have together agreed to donate their samples to biobanks for the purpose of medical research are an example of such a group. The Human Genome Organisation (HUGO) has recognized that prior consultation, communication and the acquisition of broad consent from such groups is an essential prerequisite to population-wide genomic research. Collective models of governance such as this are designed to protect the shared interests of such groups; however, they presume that these groups are a 'unitary entity' in much the same way that the 'family covenant' model of stewardship considers 'the family' to be the appropriate 'unit of care' for shared genetic information. Models of this sort will, though, prove inadequate, as bioethicist Heather Widdows notes,[15] if individual members of the group don't agree or if they have divergent or conflicting views on the worth or purpose of genetic research. In the absence of consensus within the group, it is common for researchers to seek consent from a 'culturally appropriate authority', a father figure or tribal chief, for example. But is it appropriate for such leaders to consent on behalf of subordinated minorities within the group – for example, women or children – who may object, or for whom future research might raise additional concerns? Would that constitute a kind of ethical paternalism? On the other hand, should all members of a group be excluded from a familial genetics research study simply because one member objects? Such questions are the subject of ongoing debate.

Genetic material collected from populations, including isolated indigenous communities, has proved to be an extremely valuable resource for genomic research. Sequence information derived from such studies has been employed to establish variation in the genetic profiles of different racial and ethnic groups, and has been used to determine the role that such variations can play in predisposition or resistance to disease, as well as in other political projects including the establishment of lineages, routes of migration, rates of mortality, consanguinity and the like. While the scientific and commercial utility of such studies are uncontested, the question of who should have rights of property in the genetic material (or bioinformation), or associated rights to dictate the terms of its use, remains largely unresolved. Large collections of samples and the cell lines created from them have been banked by specialist research institutes such as the American Type Culture Collection and even by national biobanking authorities. As a result, these institutions have generated property rights in, and to, the bioinformation they hold.

The fact that this bioinformation was effectively 'mined' from samples provided by indigenous communities located in some of the world's least developed countries has invoked unfavourable comparisons with historical practices of colonial exploitation. A new term 'biocolonialism' was formulated to convey concerns that this valuable resource would be expropriated to the metropolitan centres of the West and there capitalized upon in ways that would offer few economic or political benefits to the communities from which it was extracted. Serious objections to the practice have been raised by indigenous rights groups and their advocates, such as Rural Advancement Foundation International (RAFI), which argue that, aside from abrogating those communities' rights to control how their genetic resources are circulated and used, the practice also converts their cultural and biological heritage into saleable property.[16] The fact that the information could also be used by states to actively undermine important territorial or social claims advanced by such groups, for example to land rights or rights to cultural property, have only served to exacerbate their distrust. Corporate models of governance attempt to capture the principle that some groups, such as indigenous communities, may need to be treated as a 'corporate body' whose interests are more than the sum of those expressed by its individual members. Protecting those might involve, for example, preventing research using their bioinformation that could compromise the group's cultural integrity or continued existence over time.

Invention or Discovery?

In this chapter, we have so far examined how human materials, including tissue samples, saliva and blood, have been collected and transformed into biotechnological inventions to which individuals and companies can make successful property claims on the basis of the work and skill expended in their manufacture. But what occurs when the resource in question is not manufactured per se, but is simply discovered? How is it possible to exert property claims when the resource remains in its 'natural' state and has not been combined with any admixture of either physical or intellectual labour or been consequently transformed in any meaningful way? Such questions first arose in the mid-1990s as scientists began to identify the existence of a host of previously uncharacterized genes. At that time, both the US Patent Act and the European Patent Convention contained clauses that disallowed the patenting of discoveries. As genes have always existed in nature, it seemed self-evident that any work to reveal their existence would constitute an act of discovery rather than invention. However, both statutes limited their exclusions to discoveries *as such*. This proved to be an important distinction, since interpretations of US and European law determined that an invention that makes *some practical use* of a discovery can be patented, given that this is more than a discovery, *as such*. This 'practical use' was said to include even the act of isolating genes from the tissue in which they were embedded.[17]

Great controversy arose over the kind of work that was involved in isolating genes. Opponents of gene patenting argued that isolating genes was simple discovery given that it was impossible to establish the existence of genes *without* isolating them from their natural surroundings. Advocates argued, conversely, that isolating genes was not mere 'discovery' since it involved the development and application of sophisticated technical processes. The isolation of genes was an inventive act, they reasoned, because it involved taking an inventive concept (the idea of isolating a gene) and thereafter reducing it to practice, in other words, demonstrating through applied experiment that isolation was workable. It was via such reasoning that the European Patent Convention determined in 2008 that 'an element isolated from the human body or otherwise produced by means of a technical process, including sequences or partial sequences of a gene, may constitute a patented invention *even if the structure of that element is identical to that of a natural element*' (our italics).[18] The same argument was later employed to substantiate intellectual property right (IPR) claims to genetic sequences and bioinformation stored on electronic databases. Both the sequences and the databases were declared to be inventions because they had been generated through the implementation of an applied technical process, although the latter, due to their informational form, became eligible to be copyrighted as specific compilations of data rather than as patented works. While legal cases such as these can seem rather dry, if not arcane, they proved to have a profound effect on the way bioinformation has come into being as both an available and an extremely valuable resource for the biotechnology and biomedical research industries. Nowhere is the impact of such decisions better illustrated than in the Myriad Genetics case.

Myriad: Patenting Breast Cancer Genes

Breast cancer is one of the leading causes of death in women worldwide. While there are identifiable environmental antagonists for breast cancer, some women are at greater risk due to their genetic make-up. BRCA-1 and BRCA-2 are genes that express a protein in the cells of breast tissue that helps to repair damaged DNA and ensure normal cell growth. When these genes are mutated, their ability to carry out these repairs is disrupted. Women who carry such mutations thus have much higher susceptibility for disease, currently numbering between 5 per cent and 10 per cent of all those with breast cancer and 15 per cent of all those with ovarian cancer. These women can, however, mitigate their risk of contracting such diseases by taking preventative steps, which include screening, medication and pre-emptive surgery. To know that they are at risk, they must first undergo a genetic test to determine the presence or absence of the BRCA-1 and BRCA-2 genes.

During the 1990s, Myriad Genetics, a private molecular diagnostics company in the United States, filed for patents on these mutated genes, claiming that they had been the first to identify their location and sequence. Researchers working in publicly funded institutions who had also played a key role in the identification of these genes robustly contested this history of events, but were nevertheless unsuccessful in blocking Myriad's patent claims. In developing diagnostic tests for the mutations, Myriad had both isolated out the BRCA-1 and BRCA-2 mutations (genomic DNA, or gDNA) and created complementary DNA (cDNA), which is a synthetic version of the original that lacks the noncoding regions normally found within it. Patent claims were made on both, and were successfully obtained. In determining that they were both Myriad's inventions, the court effectively granted the company an exclusive right to control how those processes and the genes involved would be utilized over the following 20-year period of the patent term.

Having secured the right to isolate BRCA genes and to create BRCA cDNA, Myriad was able to create a monopoly on the production of diagnostic gene testing kits. Although they did not have a patent on BRCA diagnostic kits per se, they were able to take action against competitors who tried to create rival kits, given that it was impossible to do this without first isolating or creating synthetic BRCA DNA, an act that infringed Myriad's process patents. Although rival producers of test kits, doctors, patients and advocacy groups all contested Myriad's patents, they were unsuccessful, as a result of which Myriad became the sole commercial provider of testing kits and services for identification of the BRCA-1 and BRCA-2 mutations in the United States, including its flagship product, the BRACAnalysis® test.

An extremely asymmetrical set of power relations emerged out of this particular marketization of the BRCA genes and the bioinformation derived from them. In order to isolate the mutations, it was first necessary to acquire samples of tissue from women in families with very high incidences of breast cancer. This work was initially undertaken by Mary-Claire King, then a geneticist working at the University of California, Berkeley. Many, if not all, of the women who donated did so in order to establish whether there was a genetic link between breast cancer and ovarian cancer, but they also did so in order to help develop tests and therapeutics to aid early detection and treatment of these potentially fatal conditions. However, once Myriad had secured patents on the genes, it began to aggressively enforce its monopoly rights, sending 'cease and desist' notices to all those using the BRCA genes without licence, including even academics using them in non-applied research. Myriad's ability to exclude other commercial producers of the test enabled it to charge US$3,000–4,000 for a single diagnostic test, compared to their competitors projected costs of US$1,000–2,300.

The economic and social implications of this monopoly were striking for donor families and their extended network of relatives. Despite having contributed the essential genetic raw material, they had become effectively priced out of the market for tests that were essential for diagnosis of risk. Advocacy groups were outraged, with one genetic counsellor arguing that levying inflated charges amounted to 'collecting blood money off my patients'.[19] The BRACAnalysis® test certainly became hugely profitable for Myriad, earning the company over US$400 million per year, which dramatically increased their revenue stream between 2004 and 2012 (see figure 3.1). The company's decision to market the test kits 'direct to consumer' via the post raised further ethical concerns that the test would be aggressively marketed both to women who were at relatively low risk (simply in order to obtain more genetic data) and to vulnerable 'at-risk' women who would not have access to necessary support services, such as genetic counselling, post diagnosis.

As legal commentators A. Lane Baldwin and Robert Cook-Deegan have astutely noted, Myriad was not the only company to hold patents on isolated human genes at this time; many other companies, such as Genentech, also had extensive portfolios.[20] What distinguished Myriad's business practices was the proprietorial approach they took to exercising those rights.

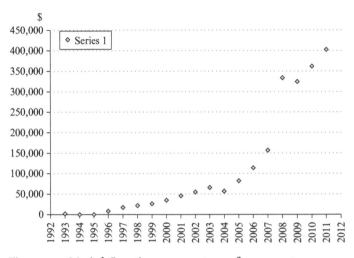

Figure 3.1   Myriad Genetics revenue stream from 1993 to 2011

Source: https://www.researchgate.net/figure/235390150_fig1_Myriad-
Genetics-revenue-stream-from-1993-to-2011-Data-derived-from-66

Unlike other corporations, they failed to form collaborative partnerships with disease communities, research scientists or advocacy groups, choosing to tightly restrict access to these valuable resources (genetic sequences and data), an ethos that quickly began to generate much public disquiet and disapproval.

Conclusion

The Moore, Lacks and Myriad cases are particularly significant as they demonstrated, for the first time, that human tissue and the information that it contains could transition from being an unownable and uncommodifiable bodily material into alienable property that can be legally bought and sold. In this chapter, we have investigated how that became possible. Making human genetic material and bioinformation available for applied use required that it be 'reworked', extracted from the donor's body and rendered in new, more stable forms – as isolated or synthesized DNA, as clones, immortalized cell lines or sequences stored on databases. This could not be achieved without appropriate investments of skill and expertise, and physical and intellectual labour on the part of research scientists, institutions and corporations. A series of key legal rulings determined that intellectual property rights to these new 'works' could be granted, despite the fact that they are derived from human material, because bringing them into the world was deemed an act of manufacture or invention, not just discovery. Exclusive rights to control access to and use of these inventions are granted, through the award of patents or copyright, to individuals or corporations that are deemed to have authored the invention, as recompense for their expended labour.

It is also clear, however, that while genetic material and associated bioinformation can acquire a new identity as sophisticated pieces of biotechnological property, they have not wholly shed their previous ones – that is, as someone's former body part. This paradox underpins much of the contestation and debate that has since attended the commercialization of such material. For although there is general acceptance that such products cannot be brought to market without suitable recompense for the time and effort invested in their conception and manufacture, assigning exclusive rights to their ownership and use to the individuals or corporations that are said to have invented them has proved to be highly controversial. In the following chapter, we examine what happens when these resources begin to enter formal markets, to appear as products that users, such as the woman who sought access to Myriad's test kits, have to pay to access. Their experiences sparked a debate over how contributions to the development of these new resources should be understood and recognized, both socially and economically. Two key questions that attend the commercialization of many valuable resources – who should be considered to have rights in them and who should benefit from their commercial exploitation – proved to be equally controversial here, as the next chapter will reveal.

CHAPTER FOUR

Markets: Who Consumes Bioinformation?

Introduction

We all might, as individuals, believe that we have an inaliena-ble right to the bioinformation contained within our cells and tissues, as well as a heavily vested interest in other kinds of bioinformation – such as that held on our medical records – taken from us by health professionals. However, these rights are arguably of little use to most of us, as we lack the skills and resources to exploit this information to the benefit of either others or ourselves. Instead, we rely on scientific and medi-cal experts (as discussed in Chapter 3) to extract, process and render that information in new bioinformatic forms from which meaningful knowledge about human identity, develop-ment, health and disease can be obtained. This means that we can only benefit from our bioinformation by placing it – or allowing it to be placed – in the hands of others.

At this point bioinformation becomes a resource that can be used in a variety of non-commercial and commercial ways. Some of the people who have access to our bioinformation, such as doctors or other healthcare personnel, use it to directly inform decision-making about our individual lives. They may do so by testing for genetic markers that indicate a predis-position to disease or by using the bioinformation to predict our reaction to prescribed drugs. Others who seek to exploit bioinformation will do so in ways that will, for the most part, seemingly have little direct impact on individual donors.

Consider, for example, how medical record data is used by national healthcare systems for broader purposes of epidemiological research and healthcare surveillance and planning, how biobanks used accessioned samples to identify new targets for the development of drugs or diagnostic tools, or how forensic bioinformation is used for surveillance purposes that may, in fact, even work against the donor's interests.

In this chapter, we develop some of the arguments made about ownership in Chapter 3 by thinking through the question of who could or should benefit from the circulation, exchange and commercialization of bioinformation. First, we outline the different ways in which bioinformation is mobilized and put to use: who makes use of bioinformation and for what purposes? We start by looking at individual genetic testing, before turning to consider how larger-scale genetic resources and biobanks are used for the purposes of public health planning, forensic science and medical and scientific research. Second, we explore the burgeoning global market for bioinformation, examining how bioinformation is mobilized and commodified. Finally, we ask who benefits from the research carried out using bioinformation and, in particular, whether the benefits reach those who originally donated the data.

Putting Bioinformation to Use

Individual genetic testing

For individuals, bioinformation is increasingly becoming an everyday part of healthcare provision, especially in more economically developed countries. As we saw in Chapter 2, Guthrie cards (newborn blood spots) are now routinely taken at birth and used to screen babies for a range of common but serious diseases that need to be treated rapidly after birth, including PKU, hypothyroidism and CF. Advances in screening techniques, including Tandem Mass Spectrometry (TMS) and DNA chip technology, mean that an even wider range of disorders may be effectively screened for in the near future. Families or communities with a known history of a particular disease may also seek out genetic screening to help inform their health behaviours. One well-known example is that of actress Angelina Jolie, who discovered through genetic testing that she carried a mutation of the BRCA-1 gene, which placed her at increased risk of developing breast cancer. Jolie opted to have a double mastectomy to mitigate the risk. In the United Kingdom, her decision sparked a wave of requests for testing for breast cancer, which became known as the 'Angelina Jolie effect'.[1]

Genetic testing may also be used to inform decisions about starting a family. Within the Ashkenazi Jewish community, there is a higher prevalence of Tay-Sachs disease, an inherited disorder. Children born with Tay-Sachs experience a rapid slow-down in development, and most die before they reach the age of 4. If both prospective parents carry the genetic mutation associated with the disease, there is a 25 per cent chance that any child of theirs will have the condition. In the United Kingdom, the National Health Service (NHS) offers screening for parents and pregnant couples in high-risk groups. Testing is also associated with genetic counselling, which offers advice to those tested on how to interpret, make sense of and act on the knowledge (for instance, of disease risk) generated using their bioinformation. This is an important requirement if the value of the resource is to be fully realized. Without it, those who seek testing may arrive at inaccurate conclusions about the implications of a positive result, a matter to which we will return, in respect of commercial genetic testing.

Biobanks and gene-discovery research
Associations such as that found between BRCA-1 and BRCA-2 genes and breast cancer are usually derived from

research using larger-scale biobanks, such as those described in Chapter 2. This kind of research involves using statistical techniques to 'mine' the collections of information held within biobanks for links between genes and diseases. Some collections of bioinformation, including many held by hospitals and medical research institutions, tend to focus on specific diseases or conditions. For example, the Manchester Cancer Research Centre focuses on collecting samples from patients with suspected cancer or those undergoing cancer treatment.[2] These kinds of disease-based databases were key to creating some of the earliest discovered links between genes and diseases. If we take, for example, the discovery of the genetic mutation linked to Huntington's disease, the first disease-associated gene to be molecularly mapped to a human chromosome,[3] we discover that the bioinformation used to conduct the study was originally sourced from just two large families with a history of the disease. Prominent Huntington's disease researcher Nancy Wexler, whose interest in the field had been motivated by her own family history of the disease, began the collection of genetic material by identifying families with a very high predisposition to the condition. In *Mapping Fate*,[4] her personal memoir of the search for the gene for Huntington's, Wexler's sister Alice describes how Nancy tracked down two Venezuelan communities living near Lake Maracaibo with high incidences of Huntington's, and another large Huntington's disease-affected family located near Ohio.

By combining the genetic, genealogical and medical information that she obtained from these families, Wexler effectively created a biobank resource that enabled herself and her team (over a period of more than 20 years) to map the Huntington's disease gene and develop a prenatal and presymptomatic test for the condition. This was a major breakthrough, as Huntington's is usually asymptomatic until those affected are between 30 and 50 years of age. Interestingly, both Nancy and Alice Wexler chose not to undertake the test to establish whether they carried the gene. Their decision reflects some of the complex and life-altering implications of acquiring the kinds of genetic knowledge that a reading of one's bioinformation can provide. It is often assumed that the greater transparency and legibility of one's prospective fate that might be derived from such an analysis is always beneficial to the patient; however, this may not be the case, especially when the disease in question is untreatable. In such instances, the benefits of 'not knowing' may considerably outweigh those of knowing.

Larger national biobanks, by contrast, have wider remits and tend to recruit much more diverse cohorts of donors. UK Biobank, for example, cites its aim as being to improve the 'prevention, diagnosis and treatment of a wide range of serious and life-threatening illnesses – including cancer, heart diseases, stroke, diabetes, arthritis, osteoporosis, eye disorders, depression and forms of dementia'.[5] This wider remit creates important economies of scale in the collection and processing of accessions, allowing large, well characterized banks of material to be created for a variety of research uses. There are a number of reasons why this is advantageous. First, given the wide range and scope of diseases, it is simply not practical to establish a unique biobank (as Wexler did) for every known health concern or disorder. Second, changes in technology also mean that, while the cost of DNA sequencing and analysis has fallen dramatically, as seen in the recent announcement of the US$1,000 genome,[6] finding links between genes and diseases, followed by developing appropriate treatments, remains a very costly process and one with a high rate of failures. The cost of new drug development has been calculated to be in excess of US$1 billion, with estimates of a 95 per cent failure rate for creating a new drug.[7] Third, and relatedly, most diseases, disorders and health concerns are both complex and multifactorial. Huntington's is, in this sense, exceptional in so far as it proves to be a condition that is caused by a mutation in a single gene. The majority of diseases are, conversely, caused by a combination of multiple genetic and environmental factors. Understanding the associations between them and identifying possible causal relationships and, ultimately, effective treatments and interventions require detailed bioinformation (samples, genetic data and medical records) from much larger cohorts than those found in Wexler's study.

This combination of economies of scale, the costs of research and the complexity of gene–disease–environment associations is primarily what shapes the large-scale national, international and commercial biobanks that today dominate bioinformatics research. Biobanks are often not research projects in and of themselves (although they may be home to several large cohort studies), but serve, rather, as resources for a wider public and private sector research community. The research community, through either academic collaborations or commercial partnerships, negotiate access to bioinformation for the purposes of asking specific research questions about associations between genes, disease and environment. The information held in biobanks can be used to indicate who is at risk of developing a disease, to isolate genetic markers linked to that disease, to develop drugs to target their effects or to identify particular 'at risk' individuals for treatment. The samples that they provide are, in this respect, understood as a kind of 'public resource' that any suitably qualified researcher can access. Consequently, participants in biobanks, unlike individuals who undertake personalized or commercial genetic testing, are generally unlikely to receive any direct feedback about their health status, even if that status is found to be seriously compromised in the course of research using the biobank's data.

Bioinformation and public health

The relationships between genes, diseases and treatments found by 'mining' biobanks can also be used to inform public health decision-making. In particular, there is a strong interest in developing more personalized approaches to disease, diagnosis and treatment based on pharmacogenomics – studies that explore how an individual's genetic characteristics influence their response to pharmaceutical products. An early example of how this might work in practice was seen in the UK in their use of bioinformation to determine access to Herceptin, a breast cancer treatment.[8] Early trials confirmed this drug's utility in arresting tumour spread, but only in those women with a particular form of breast cancer known as HER-2. In 2000, the UK National Institute of Health and Clinical Excellence (NICE), which decides which drugs should be funded through the NHS, licensed Herceptin for the treatment of advanced breast cancer, but only to those patients who were proven to have the HER-2 form of the disease, just 20–30 per cent of all those with breast cancer. This use of bioinformation (about HER-2 status) to determine access to treatment proved highly controversial and was robustly contested by those deemed untreatable with this drug. The ethics of arriving at judgements on access to care purely on the basis of generalized genetic predictions is discussed in greater detail in Chapter 5.

Equally controversial have been attempts to link drug allocation to racial profiles. In the absence of a system that can quickly sequence individual genomes in the clinical setting, pharmaceutical developers are instead trying to develop drugs that target populations seen as genetically 'distinctive'. In this way, race has come to be viewed as a legitimate proxy for significant genetic variation in drug response. In 2005, the US regulatory body for approving new medicines, the Food and Drug Administration (FDA), approved BiDil, a drug for severe heart failure that works by relaxing blood vessels, thus making it easier for the heart to pump. An initial application for approval of the drug made in 1997 was denied because the FDA felt the original study, conducted by Jay N. Cohn, a University of Minnesota cardiologist, provided insufficient evidence of efficacy in a general population.[9] However, a retrospective review of this original study did find evidence that some African American patients could potentially benefit from BiDil.[10] The potential market for this new drug was very significant, as African American patients have a statistically higher risk of death from heart failure than their white counterparts. The commercial firm, NitroMed, decided to trial the drug again looking only at its effect on African American patients. Their study found that those given BiDil had significantly better outcomes than those given a placebo, paving the way for the drug's approval.[11] NitroMed then began to market the drug by specifically targeting doctors known to treat African American patients.

In many respects, this tailoring of drugs to racially defined patients can be seen as a positive development, as it enables the recovery of pharmaceuticals previously 'lost' in the development process due to the identification of adverse drug reactions (ADRs). If it can be proven that drugs that have failed clinical trials have done so only because they produced ADRs in certain subgroups of the population, there is a possibility that they could be safely rehabilitated for use by others, thereby increasing the range of overall treatment options. One recent advance in the field of cancer has been the use of genetic screening of tumours for patients with advanced or rare cancers who have often exhausted all available treatment options. Tumour screening allows medical professionals to match these patients with phase one clinical trials aimed at 'rescuing' previously rejected treatments by showing that those treatments are effective in a subgroup of the population whose tumours have certain molecular mutations.[12]

The targeting and approval of drugs for particular *racial* groups is, however, viewed by many in a more negative light. The concern is that such practices further sediment the reification of racial categories in the provision of healthcare, which in turn invites or legitimates stigmatization. As we will show in Chapter 5, creating perceptual associations between race and particular kinds of disease can create a kind of 'predictive shortcut' that may look robust, but is, in fact, far from it in practice. All manner of commercial enterprises that have interests in assessing risk (from medical insurers to employment agencies) can draw conclusions about the likelihood that people of different racial groups will, or will not, suffer from certain health conditions on the basis of a generalized profile that takes little or no account of individual diversity.

The inclusion of racial criteria in the construction of some larger biobanks, such as the US NIH's HapMap project,[13] has also invoked concerns that wider biomedical research could soon be oriented towards the identification of diseases, the distribution of which is either said to be, or perhaps just constructed to be, organized along racial lines. The implication of this for drug marketing can be significant and troublesome. African American activists and researchers have noted NitroMed's co-option of the Association of Black Cardiologists to help organize their clinical research and subsequent marketing of BiDil. NitroMed's main motivation for their study was not, they suggest, benevolence; nor was it a desire to redress inequalities in the focus of drug research and development. Rather, it was the identification of a significant African American market for heart disease treatment. The fact that heart disease disproportionally affects Africa Americans is arguably an effect of earlier discrimination and racial inequality in the United States, a history that some consider it unjust to benefit from. The risk with the racial and socio-economic profiling of disease is that research and development into

new medicines will target the so-called 'diseases of afflu-
ence' whose sufferers have the resources to pay, while other
diseases, which afflict poorer racial or ethnic minorities,
will become neglected or 'orphaned' as the market for their
consumption is viewed as limited. Genetic profiling is not,
however, only limited to the domain of health and biomedical
research: it has also become a key technique in policing and
surveillance work.

Forensic uses of bioinformation
In a 2008 paper, Amade M'charek reveals how the creation of
DNA databases has transformed the way in which DNA evidence is now used in criminal investigations.[14] Initially, DNA
evidence was used to link a sample from a suspect already
identified in the course of an investigation to DNA traces left
at the scene of a crime, much like Henry Elliot's fingerprints
were (see Chapter 1). The huge expansion and availability
of forensic DNA databases (those generated by police and
enforcement agencies worldwide) is such that it is now possible to compare traces of DNA found at the scene of a crime
with some of the millions of genetic profiles held worldwide,
making them an invaluable resource for crime detection and
terrorism prevention.

Using bioinformation to identify the race or ethnicity of a
suspect can have positive effects; it can be used to exonerate
suspect populations who are often disproportionately blamed
for crimes in a given locality. The UK-based Nuffield Council
on Bioethics has, though, also drawn attention to 'mission
creep' in relation to the construction and forensic use of both
police and other DNA databases.[15] As we go on to highlight
in the following chapters, the ability to use collected bioinformation to solve crime can be very seductive, leading operators
to overreach the conditions of the databases' establishment.
The practice of familial searching, for example, has proven

highly controversial, as it involves police operatives searching the database for those whose DNA profiles suggest a genetic link to the suspect. While this usually means the identification of a close known relative, such as a brother or son, it can sometimes reveal the existence of previously unknown familial connections between subjects. This activity becomes even more contentious when samples are compared with DNA databases that were not even created for forensic use. Other kinds of genetic research undertaken on samples held in forensic databases is even more dubious – for example, studies purporting to reveal racial predispositions to criminality. The fact that such research is unconsented and not subject to normal processes of ethical review has attracted much criticism, for, although methodologically and ethically flawed, it can nevertheless be used to unfairly stigmatize those minority populations that are already overrepresented in the database.

Caution is also needed when thinking about the ability of non-experts, including both legal professionals and juries, to make sense of DNA evidence. If we compare the media representations and portrayals of DNA evidence on popular shows such as the American TV drama *Crime Scene Investigation*, we can see a tendency to equate DNA evidence with certainty, when in fact – as we noted above in the case of medical genetic testing – making sense of bioinformation necessitates considerable expertise. The growth and progressive linkage of forensic databases internationally, including important new technological advances that greatly increase what is known as their 'interoperability', is extending the optics of surveillance in unprecedented ways – and with it the global market for these new bioinformational resources. Threats (whether from contagious diseases or terrorist actions) are legitimating the collection of an array of biometric data at every national border in circumstances and under conditions that prove all but impossible to protest. The threat of deportation is enough to prompt willing acquiescence to the process of iris scanning or fingerprint capture, while the need to contain Ebola provides enough justification for most to collect personal health information or submit to temperature scanning. These strategies, alongside more covert forms of analysis such as use of social media and search engine data for signs of epidemic outbreaks and other health trends, reflect how bioinformation is being enrolled into wider biosecurity agendas, and made complicit in the prosecution of states' geopolitical goals. The question of where such data goes, and how it is swept up, consolidated and later used remains, however, a mystery to most. Such developments nevertheless invite us to reflect on how bioinformation is put to work as a resource for distinguishing 'us' from 'them' in the wider, but very contentious, political project of identifying potential 'threats' to national security.

Commercializing Bioinformation

All of these uses inevitably involve the commodification of bioinformation. The value of bioinformation to each of these markets is very difficult to fully determine as its invisibility as a resource means that it is only rarely identified as a 'raw material' per se and costed as such. Some broad figures can, however, give a meaningful estimation of what a vital resource bioinformation is to a variety of emergent economies and companies. In 2015, the commercial online genetic testing company 23andMe raised US$115 million of venture capital financing from partners, including Google Ventures, New Enterprise Associates, Casdin Capital and WuXi Healthcare Ventures, to support its new consumer product range and the development of drug discovery informed by its huge genetic database.[16] Financiers speculate that this implies a company valuation of US$1.1 billion. The biotechnology forecaster BioWorld has revealed the dramatic expansion of the DNA

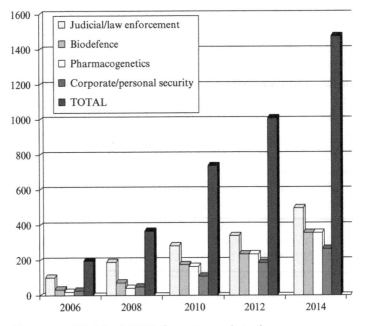

Figure 4.1   Worldwide DNA forensics market value, 2005–14

Source: BioWorld, Clarivate Analytics (www.bioworld.com)

forensics market that has occurred since the early 2000s, which propelled the judicial and law enforcement segment to grow from a US$103.9 million market in 2006 to a US$494.6 million one in 2014. The biodefence market for personal data, DNA sequences and technologies has grown similarly, from US$41.3 million in 2006 to over US$356 million in 2014. Meanwhile, the pharmacogenetics market, driven by increasing interest in personalized medicine, is also now valued in excess of US$350 million (see figure 4.1).[17]

The translation of personal information and genetic samples into what sociologist of science Mary Ebeling calls 'biodata commodities'[18] has raised a series of social and ethical concerns. As we saw in Chapter 2, many cultures have aversions to the practice of bodily commodification, which are reflected in national policies forbidding trade in either whole persons (slavery) or their parts (including organs, tissue and cadavers). While there are some exceptions to this tradition, seen in the establishment of legal markets in 'renewable' bodily substances such as sperm and blood in the United States and in the operation of grey markets in kidneys from living donors in some other countries,[19] the norm has been one of prohibition of commercialization and the valorization of altruistic donation. Neoliberal values and agendas are argued by many to present an increasing threat to this altruistic tradition as they seek to construct donated bioinformation not as a 'gift' for collective use in the public interest, but, rather, as an industrial raw material that can be more effectively capitalized on when privatized. It is important to understand both how bodily resources came to be understood as commodities that could be privately owned, and also what characterizing them in this way has invoked in terms of the changing dynamics of the distribution of profits generated from their applied use.

The privatization of bioinformational resources

Much of the shift in attitude that we have witnessed in relation to the commodification of human bodily materials had its genesis in changing approaches to the governance of other biological resources that emerged in the early 1980s as the biotechnological revolution began. Previously, the Food and Agriculture Organization (FAO) of the United Nations had declared that plant and animal materials constitute part of the 'common heritage of mankind that consequently should be available without restriction'.[20] In the biological realm, 'the commons' is a term used to refer to environmental resources: grazing lands, rivers, fisheries, etc., which are collectively owned and utilized between or among groups to their mutual benefit, and which cannot be privately owned. During the nineteenth century, this ethos came to be viewed as antithetical to capitalist production. The absence of a single property rights holder, it was argued, leaves the resource open to exploitation by the masses. Their inherently self-interested and unregulated use of the resource leads inexorably to its inevitable diminution, resulting in what the environmentalist Garrett Hardin described in his landmark 1968 work as 'the Tragedy of the Commons'.[21] In this ideological tradition, privatization provides the necessary basis for sustainable extraction of profit and, thus, wider regimes of profit accumulation.

This ethos came to inform approaches to the ownership and use of the genetic resources, the vital raw material of the biotechnology industry. The UN Conference on Biodiversity and Environment swept away the FAO's commons framework, ratifying, with the passage of the conference's Convention on Biological Diversity (CBD) in 1993,[22] the principle that genetic materials (of plant, animal or microbial derivation) would form part of a nation-state's patrimony that it is free to commercialize at will. This determination had quite profound consequences, validating a model that actively promoted the privatization of genetic and bioinformational resources. Interestingly, although human genetic materials stood outside the remit of the CBD, they soon became similarly characterized as alienable commodities within the biotechnology industry. The *Diamond v. Chakrabarty* case (outlined in Chapter 3) that had legitimated patents on modified biological products later converged with the World Trade Organization's (WTO) Trade Related Intellectual Property Rights (TRIPS) agreement to make acceptance of biological patenting a condition of valuable international trade agreements. Together, they combined to sediment a belief that the value of genetic and bioinformational resources could only be realized via the granting of private property rights.

As we explored in Chapter 3, the ability to translate human bodily parts (cells, tissue, proteins and genetic sequences) into new technological products such as cell lines and sequence databases later provided the rationale for treating these as inventions that could, similarly, be privately owned. Privatization was, however, to be balanced by the introduction of new benefit sharing regimes: agreements designed to ensure that donated bioinformational resources were collected with suitably informed consent and that the resulting benefits – whether financial or social – be shared equitably among all donors. Although this principle was widely promoted by the pharmaceutical industry in the collection of plant, animal and microbial samples and bioinformation, the same could not be said of human-derived resources. This was probably a consequence of a continuing disavowal of the fact that bodily commodification was actually occurring. Manufacturing tissue into new products such as databases or cell lines generates a 'psychic distance' between these products and the individuals from whom they are drawn, allowing these resources to be viewed, as anthropologist Margaret Lock puts it, as 'thing-like, as non-self, and detachable from the body without causing irreparable loss or damage to the individual or generations to follow'.[23] As long as it appeared that fleshy human bodily material itself was not being commercialized, no benefits or compensation needed to be offered.

Maintaining this particular fiction became increasingly difficult as the market for human tissue and bioinformation began to grow and as reports of the commercialization of such resources reached the public domain. The Moore, Lacks and Myriad cases (discussed in Chapter 3) were pivotal because they demonstrated that individuals' tissues, DNA and bioinformation were being crudely mined without consent and commercialized in ways that allowed profits to be monopolized exclusively by the property rights holder. Although donors had provided the 'raw' bioinformatic material, they were not viewed as having contributed any knowledge or expertise to the creation of the invented products, and were thus not considered entitled to any financial gain. Concerns about the fundamental inequity of this situation led to calls to extend benefit sharing models to the collection and use of human genetic resources and bioinformation.

As we shall demonstrate in the following sections, establishing how to distribute such benefits and to whom, or even agreeing what constitutes a benefit, has proven immensely complex. Benefits were initially rather narrowly construed as simply monetary profits, a conception that has been widened more recently to include 'public goods' such as improved testing and treatment regimes, improved medical research or the creation of publicly accessible bioinformational databases. Some commentators have questioned the rationale for benefit sharing, arguing, as Ruth Chadwick and Kåre Berg have done,[24] that the aim may simply be to 'buy' acquiescence rather than to secure distributive justice, or, as Kadri Simm suggests,[25] just to legitimize commercialization and profit seeking behaviour. The question of how to weigh the value of each contributor's input (is a scientist's input worth more than a donor's or other medical staff?) has exercised policymakers and academics alike and has yet to be satisfactorily resolved.[26] Cases such as that involving the Hagahai (discussed in Chapter 3), where the tissue or bioinformation concerned has population-wide significance, raise particular challenges in terms of consent and the potential disbursement of benefits. From whom and to whom should consent and compensation be sought and offered: the individual donor, the whole tribe or, following the principles of the CBD, the nation-state? Such concerns are amplified as the scale of collections increases and as the degree of interoperability between collections (linkages and sharing across platforms) intensifies. New approaches to the accessing and sharing of 'big data' and models for the distribution of potential benefits are outlined and assessed in Chapters 5 and 6.

Public and private interests in biobanking
The question of how and with whom to share the potential benefits of the commercialization of large collections of bio-informational data has long been an issue (as illustrated in the case of deCODE Genetics, discussed in Chapter 2) and is becoming increasingly acute as the distinction between public biobanking practices (that rely on altruistic donation) and commercial private sector biobanking begins to collapse. Public biobanks – like UK Biobank – are increasingly looking into what they might be able to offer participants in exchange for their participation, including the feedback of relevant information on their health and wellbeing. Corporate biobankers, like deCODE, view these kinds of publicly held bodies of bioinformation as not only very valuable, but also, in their view, underutilized resources. As a result, they seek to create alliances with them in order to 'mine' their collections. Private sector involvement is arguably motivated by the potentially lucrative rewards to be gained from securing licensed access to biobanked resources, which are, typically, highly characterized. This means that the accessioned samples are accompanied by very detailed data about donors, their health status, previous illnesses, family history of disease, lifestyle, behaviour and the like. The ability to fully interrogate the genetics of a sample in light of the lived and environmental experience of its donor is invaluable. As we noted in Chapter 2, it is here that provenance comes into play. Commercial pharmaceutical developers would struggle to locate new targets for drugs and treatments or be able to identify new pharmaceutical markets, such as those associated with particular racial

groups as previously discussed, without being able to access resources of this quality.

Custodians of public sector biobanks view such approaches with a certain degree of ambivalence. Supporters suggest that private sector involvement is essential because it secures the high level of financial investment necessary to construct the bank and protect its future operations. This, they argue, is particularly so for smaller or more specialized banks, which would otherwise struggle to survive. Some suggest that it might even be appropriate to incentivize commercial company involvement by offering them exclusive rights to profit from products generated using the sponsored bank's data. Similar approaches are being championed for other larger banks such as the UK Biobank and Generation Scotland. While data will be held under the stewardship of these biobank's research governing bodies, it has been envisioned that private companies could also be given access for research purposes and be granted exclusive intellectual property rights to products they develop from that research. Critics have been incensed by such suggestions, drawing attention to the inequity involved in allowing private corporations to profit exclusively from accessions donated in the public interest. Many of those who contributed samples and data to Iceland's Health Sector Database, were, for example, deeply troubled by the fact that deCODE Genetics (a commercial enterprise) was able to obtain an exclusive licence to access the database. A key issue of concern for such participants was that exclusivity would in fact reduce, rather than expand, the scope of research performed on these resources.

Another well-known dispute over access to bioinformation is that described by anthropologist Paul Rabinow in his book *French DNA*.[27] The book focuses on debates that took place in Paris in 1994 over a proposed collaboration between the French research laboratory, the Centre d'Étude

du Polymorphisme Humain (CEPH), well known for producing the first physical map of the human genome), and
venture capital-funded American start-up biotechnology company, Millennium Pharmaceuticals. The collaboration was
designed to establish whether there is a genetic basis for non-
insulin-dependent forms of diabetes. Such a link would have
important implications for public health, as well as offering
a potentially lucrative new target for drug development. This
example is of interest because the proposed collaboration highlights the range of resources, funding and expertise needed
to fully exploit bioinformatic resources. While researchers at
CEPH had generated a hugely valuable bioinformatic resource
in the form of a large collection of samples and bioinformation drawn from participating families – some of whom
had long histories of non-insulin-dependent diabetes – they
lacked the technical means to investigate it fully. Millennium
Pharmaceuticals provided faster and more powerful technologies for gene identification and extensive research funding at
a time when French science was facing budget cutbacks. It is
interesting to note that the proposed collaboration eventually
collapsed because the French government blocked the deal,
citing concerns that the project was effectively giving away a
precious national resource: French DNA.

What happens, then, if rather than relying on altruistic donation 'for the greater good', biobanks instead offer something
in exchange for an individual's bioinformation? This model is
exemplified by the Direct-to-Consumer genetic testing company 23andMe, which offers what appears to be a mutually
beneficial exchange: their expertise in interpreting your bioinformation in exchange for your sample and the modest sum
of US$125. However, what is actually being acquired and later
traded by 23andMe is an enormous database of highly characterized bioinformation, creating the company's own private
biobank that those in commercial biopharmaceutical research

will later 'pay-to-view'. These companies can then, as noted above, use the data to identify individuals at risk and genetic targets for drug and other therapeutic interventions. In a commercial context, these bodies of information represent two significant opportunities: promising lines of inquiry for the development of new drugs or healthcare products, and an already-identified population of at-risk individuals who could form the market for such interventions.

Opinion surveys conducted to date suggest that the public has mixed responses to the prospect of commercialization, ranging from ambivalence to reluctance and suspicion. Interestingly, focus groups conducted with participants in the Generation Scotland national genetic database in 2004 found that those groups made up of patients, activists and their supporters tended to be more willing than others to accept commercial involvement in biobank research as a necessary evil. The growing co-option of such individuals to the 'citizen science' projects of pharmaceutical development and big data initiatives, which directly recruit patients and sponsor associated support groups, websites and blogs, may be working to soften their view of the role and motivations of commercial companies. Certainly, those with little or no personal experience of disease, pharmaceutical development or clinical trials 'tended to construct a "public = good; private = bad" equation, viewing commercial involvement as acceptable only when profit sharing feeds benefits directly back to the community'.[28] Delivering this would require that commercial users develop a model for benefit sharing before being granted access to any public biobank. While such proposals appear to have the potential to resolve much of the conflict over the distribution of profits from the applied use of collected bioinformation, they also raise a final set of questions that we will explore next: what form can 'benefits' take and to whom should they be distributed?

Distributing the Benefits of Bioinformation

Having looked at some of the many ways in which bioinformation is being exploited as a commercial resource, we now turn to consider how the benefits that arise from this exploitation could or should be distributed. First, it is important to note that research success is one of the key benefits to arise out of the exploitation of bioinformation. Scientists and researchers may not always benefit financially from their work, but high-quality research generated using bioinformation can bring prestige, publications, funding and successful careers. Consider, for example, the reputation and enormous personal wealth built up by American biochemist-geneticist J. Craig Venter, gained as a result of his role as one of the key drivers of the Human Genome Project. Venter is an exception, though, given that such benefits are not usually framed as individual achievements. The benefits of research are usually couched as something that is shared more collectively for the good of all humankind. This in turn raises questions as to what kinds of 'goods' are generated and who actually secures access to them.

Individual feedback
A key issue for individuals seeking to 'interpret' or make use of their bioinformation is their lack of skills and resources, which complicates efforts to derive meaningful knowledge from their own biodata and materials. Personal genetic screening tests, such as those used to identify carriers of particular genetic variants (e.g., those that induce Tay-Sachs disease or CF) have been designed to provide useful, personalized feedback on genetic risk. However, accepted medical wisdom is that the results of such tests should only be delivered by trained professionals who can help the patient/consumer make sense of the findings and their implications.

This is especially important given that such results rarely establish a definite causal relationship but, rather, indicate an increased probability that an individual (or their offspring) will be affected by a particular genetic condition. As noted previously, most health conditions, with the exception of single-gene disorders such as Huntington's disease, are shaped by a complex interplay of genetic, lifestyle and environmental factors, making the strength of disease–gene associations hard to establish with certainty. Despite this, many medical professionals and researchers note that patients and 'lay' consumers of bioinformation believe genetic information to be highly deterministic of health outcomes.[29] In the absence of appropriate counselling, they therefore tend to view the results of genetic tests as providing a definitive diagnosis of the presence or absence of disease.

While donations to public sector biobanks are usually made altruistically, many participants presume that either they or their community will directly benefit from any subsequent research. Some even insist (despite repeated disclaimers to the contrary) on being provided with personalized feedback on any health findings of relevance to them or their families. The UK Progress Educational Trust, for example, recently conducted a poll in Oxford on what prospective donors would like done with samples offered to the 100,000 Genomes Project. Nearly half (48 per cent) of those surveyed reported that if they had their whole genome sequenced they would want to be told anything of significance, 'all directly related findings plus all other findings, even if they may not be important to your health'; a further 38 per cent wanted to receive all 'directly related findings plus those on a small number of "serious but actionable" conditions, that are known to be important to health and that can be acted on by clinicians'.[30] It would be very difficult to deliver this in practice, as biobank research, unlike personalized genetic tests undertaken in a healthcare setting, is focused at the scale of the population or cohort and therefore rarely produces information that is detailed or identifiable enough to be used for individual diagnoses. There are also concerns about data quality, as the level of accuracy and precision is often much lower in biobank-based research precisely because it is not used for clinical assessment. There is also no facility to provide appropriate counselling to help participants make sense of any data they might receive. Biobank operators have therefore been very reluctant to 'feedback' data directly to participants, although this may be about to change.

In response to patient demand, UK Biobank has agreed to provide some forms of feedback to participants. Donors to the bank undergo a series of physical tests (blood pressure, weight, height, waist and hip circumference, lung function, bone density), and submit samples of blood and urine for analysis to establish their general health. Any abnormal assessments emerging from this are communicated to their doctor, along with the results of any laboratory tests that indicate a serious illness for which intervention is possible. The protocol also explicitly states that participants will not receive any information derived from research undertaken using their biobanked resources. This system attempts to perform two kinds of work simultaneously. By feeding back the bioinformation collected at the point of donation – which is in many ways no different from that which might be collected by their doctor as part of a routine health check – UK Biobank seeks to fulfil participants' expectations that they will in some way benefit directly, if not financially, from their participation in the study. Using doctors as a vehicle for disseminating these findings ensures that individuals have access to the expertise needed to both interpret their bioinformation and secure appropriate treatment. It is also clear that the protocol concurrently works to restrict access to the findings produced by commercial users that they view as their proprietary assets – the private databases of genetic sequence and other bioinformation that they generate through research. They are able to later collateralize these in productive ways without needing to profit share.

The reluctance of public sector or joint public–private biobanks to provide feedback can be contrasted with the case of 23andMe, for which personalized feedback and data interpretation provide a key incentive for recruiting participants to its biobank, as well as a source of ongoing revenue generation. 23andMe makes a virtue of personalized feedback, using it as a lure to participation. Whether the relatively small amount of feedback that 23andMe offers to its subscribers is a fair exchange for the potentially highly lucrative bioinformatics resource it is gaining is another matter. As one journalist's scathing review of the information received from a similar personalized genomic testing service, deCODEme, suggests, the quality of the information which was fed back was so poor as to be virtually useless.[31] 23andMe was actually banned from marketing its personal genomic tests in 2013 by the American Food and Drug Administration over concerns about the accuracy of their test results, although the company has since been granted approval to continue to offer its services, which are now also available in the United Kingdom.[32] While the majority of genetic findings that are fed back to participants have relatively little utility for individuals, they have become very valuable when aggregated at the population level, as it is here that wider trends can be discerned. The value of big data collections of this kind is immense, as we shall see in the following chapters, but none of this is either captured or distributed to the individual donors that make up each of the data points of which these huge datasets are constituted.

Community benefits
The benefits of biobanks may also be considered to extend beyond personal healthcare information. Although the

decODE Genetics' Icelandic database project drew a lot of approbation, as we saw in Chapter 2, it also delivered some important public benefits, including the creation of a new centralized medical record database, as well as the many potential improvements that future research into the prevention, diagnosis and treatment of disease could bring. Supporters of the project also noted the prestige, wealth and jobs that Iceland has attracted through the presence of a large and successful genomics firm. Yet while biobank research has produced some significant research findings – for example, decODE Genetics' identification of mutations linked to cancer and osteoporosis[33] – scholars such as Mike Fortun have been more critical of what he describes as the 'promissory' nature of genomics.[34] This, he argues, allows commercial biobanks to successfully overplay the potential future benefits of their research in order to ramp up volunteer recruitment. One Icelandic doctor described this dynamic in practice: 'It is a wonderful propaganda ... a lot of the public bought the idea ... that this database would not only take care of medical problems in Iceland, but in the rest of the world, and ... the world would be thankful to our ... little island forever.'[35]

Even when significant research using bioinformation is generated, there are no guarantees that those who supplied the data will be able to access the benefits that flow from it. If we return to the case of Henrietta Lacks (discussed in Chapter 3), we can see that there remains a clear disjuncture between donor and beneficiary: although the HeLa cell line has become a very profitable and widely used resource in biomedical research, Lack's descendants still struggle to access basic healthcare. Similarly, we saw with the Myriad case, discussed in Chapter 3, that the women who were carrying the BRCA-1 and BRCA-2 genes linked to breast cancer, and who donated their bioinformation to help develop new genetic tests and treatments, imagined that their contributions would also benefit close kin and others at high risk from the disease. However, when new genetic tests were eventually commercialized and brought to market by Myriad, monopoly patents and exclusive licensing rights meant that donors were charged exceptionally high fees to access the very treatments their bioinformation had created. Such scenarios have seen bioinformational donors reduced to what anthropologist Kaushik Sunder Rajan terms 'purely experimental subjects' who labour without the implicit social contract of reciprocity or access to benefits.[36]

Such inequities become even more pronounced in the case of research performed on indigenous populations. Colonial histories have left many indigenous populations socially, politically and economically marginalized. Many, consequently, lack access to adequate public sector healthcare and are unable to afford private care, leaving them vulnerable to ill-health and disease. Additionally, many suffer from genetic conditions that result from their geographic isolation. As we discussed in Chapter 2, communities with few immigrants, and within which most members remain, find partners and reproduce within the same narrow gene pool, often suffer from what are known as founder effects, whereby genes that are rare in the global population (including those causing disease) become amplified within their community. This genetic isolation and amplification can serve to make them valuable sources of unique genetic samples and information, making researchers keen to work with indigenous and marginalized groups. However, there is little evidence that these communities actually benefit from the research performed on them, and most view such projects with deep scepticism. For example, indigenous Australians described the Human Genome Diversity Project as a 'vampire project' designed to extract exotic DNA that would be used to create expensive pharmaceutical products they could never afford.[37] The response to indigenous and minority population concerns within the scientific community has been increased pressure to ensure the 'ethical biovalue' of bioinformation (see Chapter 2). This involves strategies both to ensure the inclusion of indigenous people and minority populations in determining what research is undertaken using their bioinformation and, more generally, to protect these populations from scientific research, even though, ironically, they are often also populations with the greatest health needs.

Fundamentally addressing the concerns of indigenous communities arguably requires a reimagining of the ways in which such bioinformation is viewed by the scientific community. Social researchers Jenny Reardon and Kim TallBear suggest we need to rethink the way in which scientists are trained, challenging what they call the 'culture of entitlement' or the implicitly colonial sense of 'ownership' that scientists feel towards the genetic material and bioinformation collections with which they work.[38] Rather than seeing indigenous bioinformation as a resource belonging to the research and scientific institutions that hold it, they suggest that indigenous bioinformation should be considered as being 'on loan', remaining the property of the individuals and communities that supplied it.

Indigenous populations are also increasingly seeking to take control of the exploitation of their genetic resources in order to ensure that any research conducted using those resources is performed in their interest. For example, in 2010 the Native American Havasupai tribe successfully challenged the repurposing of DNA samples from their community held at Arizona State University. Researchers had begun to use the DNA samples – originally collected in the 1990s for studies into diabetes – for schizophrenia and population genetic studies. Seven years of legal action against the researchers, by both individual tribal members and the tribe collectively, resulted in members being awarded a US$700,000 settlement and the remaining DNA samples being reclaimed from the university's freezer by the tribe.[39] Furthermore, new forms of biobanking are emerging in response to the issues raised by the past exploitation of indigenous DNA. For example, the Alaska Area Specimen Bank is a collaborative venture housed by the US Centre for Disease Control but managed by the Alaska Native Tribal Health Consortium (ANTHC). Research using the 500,000 specimens contained in the bank must be for community gain and receive approval from the Indian Health Service Institutional Review Board.

Conclusion

The nature of bioinformation is such that we must rely on scientific and, in some cases, corporate expertise and funding to fully realize its potential value as a source of meaningful knowledge about human identity, development, health and disease. There are, consequently, a large number of people involved in producing bioinformatics research, every one of whom may believe they are entitled to benefit from its exploitation. These can range from the original donors and their communities to medical professionals, scientists and the public and private sector institutions that collectively make sense of bioinformatic data. Whose interests are prioritized has depended historically on where and how the data was collected. Bioinformation, when collected as part of individual genetic tests, for example, was typically used to supply the donating individual with information about their disease risk. In contrast, biobanks were designed to accumulate bioinformational data that could inform research on health at the population level by revealing more general links between genetic traits and disease. These dynamics are now, however, undergoing a substantive change, as the information that individuals contribute to online genetic testing companies for genealogical or biomedical investigation is swept up, anonymized, aggregated and repackaged into 'big data'.

Such developments are collapsing distinctions between what we used to consider as either 'private' or 'public' information. As we shall see in Chapters 5 and 6, many organizations and corporate entities – from biomedical clinics to pharmaceutical companies, health informatics analysts, data brokers, credit card companies and others – are now directly profiting from the buying and selling of this new commodity of biodata. This inevitably again raises questions about data ownership, of who can or should have the right to exploit this valuable resource, and to what end or purpose. The history of the commodification of bioinformation has been a vexed one, as the practice seemingly goes against deeply held moral and ethical norms that prohibit the buying and selling of human bodies or their parts. Although exceptions exist, including the practice of slavery and the trade in human remains and body parts, the transaction of bioinformation brings a new dimension to these concerns and new complications. One is establishing exactly when, in the process of separation from the donor, the resultant information becomes constituted formally as a commodity. Early cases such as those of John Moore and Henrietta Lacks suggest that this occurs at the point of donation, when bioinformation is extracted and made available through medical and scientific interpretation. This in turn suggests that the principal beneficiaries of any commercial value generated using bioinformation, in the form of, for example, new drug targets and pharmaceutical products, should be made up of the private or public sector research institution that interpreted the data.

Such a position necessarily ignores the implicit social contract many feel they enter into as bioinformation donors, and the expectation those donors often have is that their participation in biomedical research will result in benefits to either themselves or their communities. These issues are particularly pressing for marginalized and indigenous communities, who arguably – thanks to long histories of inequality and exploitation – have the greatest health needs but remain least likely to benefit from genetic research and treatments. While these communities may not seek to benefit financially from research conducted using their data, there is arguably a strong ethical case for ensuring that they are able to access, at an affordable price, any medical benefits and products that result, as well as the right to shape future research agendas so that they are set by community needs and not just by market opportunities. Such objectives rest, of course, on the presumption that donors are informed about how their genetic data is used, and that they are able to effectively trace where their data and bioinformation go and how they are subsequently used – a presumption that is, as we shall see, increasingly under threat.

CHAPTER FIVE

The Big Data Revolution

Introduction

Personalized medicine – the idea of a treatment programme informed by, and specifically tailored to, an individual's genetic, genomic, social and environmental profile – has become a key ambition for Western medicine. Yet, somewhat ironically, in order to think small (or personalized), so the argument goes, we first need to think big. What has become known colloquially as 'big data', large-scale population databases of information on people's genomes, their environment, behaviour, background and medical history, becomes particularly attractive in this context. When combined, these very large population datasets can provide unique insights into broad trends in correlations between genes, environmental factors and disease and how these shape the everyday lives of individuals so affected. Establishing such 'associations' will, it is imagined, allow medical professionals both to match and tailor an individual's treatment to the particular symptoms, and to develop understandings of how the individual's response to that disease and its treatment are influenced by social and environmental circumstances.

A commendable goal, one might think, but we also suggest that caution is needed when giving public and private sector institutions the capacity to 'know' individuals in such intimate detail through their bioinformation. What are the commercial, political and ethical implications of the 'big data' agenda, and how might these huge banks of bioinformation and biological data be stored and used? Furthermore, will big data deliver on its promises? Can we read beyond the hope and the hype to get a realistic picture of personalized medicine and the benefits it may offer? This chapter is dedicated to exploring some of the promises and perils raised by the generation and exploitation of bioinformation on this scale.

The Big Data Agenda

There can be little doubt that a profound revolution is currently taking place in the way bioinformation and personal data are being used in healthcare. Historically, many of the datasets that provided information about health or wellbeing (such as those noting rates of hospital admission for particular conditions in a given location) were constructed at the population level. The data was often collected anonymously or was later anonymized and, as such, could not be linked directly to individual behaviour or health histories. Other sets of records that *were* individualized (such as Bertillon's filed cards of criminals' biological attributes, or clinicians' records of a patient's treatment) existed, but were not easily aggregated to population level. The extraordinary advances that have occurred in data aggregation and analytics, the tremendous growth in use of social media and the invention of a range of wearable sensor devices (such as Fitbit and Jawbone) are, however, now radically transforming these traditional dynamics of health data generation and collection. They are doing so by creating, for the first time, the ability to amass a range of exceptionally accurate records of individual health behaviour to form vast datasets of information, characterized as 'big data'.

The appearance of big data at this particular moment in time is the product of the convergence of a number of technologies, practices and capabilities. The pharmaceutical industry has been progressively accumulating massive quantities of data from clinical trials and research; state governments and healthcare providers have been digitizing patient records and securing information on patient care from health insurers; and patients themselves have learnt to upload their own biological samples and bioinformation for genetic analysis to a range of online platforms, from health and ancestry sites to social media networks. When linked together, such data creates an entirely new technology for understanding health trends at multiple levels. On the one hand, this enables the creation of very intimate but highly detailed profiles of the health behaviour of particular individuals. On the other, when amalgamated, this big data also produces very accurate pictures of wider health trends within a given population. It has also become possible to use the conclusions drawn from this aggregated data to simply *infer* what might happen to individuals – for example, to predict their risk of developing certain diseases.

The promise of such techniques in the healthcare sector is considerable, and both public and private enterprises are now investing huge sums of money in the applied use of big data. The drivers for this are both clinical and economic and are closely tied to recent developments in healthcare delivery and funding. The cost of healthcare has risen exponentially in countries such as the United States, with healthcare expenditures standing at 17.8 per cent of GDP in 2016 and predicted to rise to 19.9 per cent by 2025.[1] Traditionally, many physicians have relied on personal judgement to diagnose disease and assess the efficacy of medicines or treatments in practice. The wealth of information that the big data revolution offers has facilitated the development of new approaches, including that of evidence-based medicine. By 'crunching' very large datasets of information, it is possible to create systematic reviews of clinical data, genetic profiles and treatment outcomes that can provide more statistically robust evidence of what works and what doesn't. This can potentially deliver huge efficiencies in healthcare delivery by ensuring that patients receive more timely and accurate diagnoses and more clinically effective treatments.

Big data also has considerable application in the field of pandemic disease surveillance. During the Ebola virus outbreak in West Africa in 2014, anonymized data from 150,000 mobile phones (which are owned by even the poorest in Africa) was given by Orange Telecom in Senegal to a Swedish nongovernmental organization called Flowminder, which used it to draw up maps of population movements in the region.[2] These maps were then used to inform decisions on the placement of treatment centres and roadblocks. The US Centre for Disease Control and Prevention (CDC) has similarly used mobile phone activity data to map the frequency and location of calls to medical helplines to help triage the flow of medical resources on the ground. During the US flu pandemic of 2012/13, Twitter agreed to allow health researchers at Johns Hopkins University to scan billions of tweets to identify and track the spread of flu infections in New York City. Using sophisticated statistical methods based on language processing technologies, the researchers were able to filter out tweets signalling concern about getting the flu from those that actually said 'I have the flu'. By linking these highly sophisticated data mining algorithms directly to the tweeter's geolocation via their smart phone, it became possible to chart the spread of the epidemic.[3]

Many commentators believe that big data will become the most valuable resource for the contemporary healthcare industry in the twenty-first century. The US NIH, for example, planned to invest US$102 million in 2016 in their big data programmes aimed at facilitating the sharing and protection of data among researchers across the nation.[4] An indication of big data's increasing commercial value can be gleaned by looking at the global market for electronic health records, which was estimated to be worth in excess of US$22 billion in 2015.[5] It is not only formal economies, though, that value bioinformation. Cybercriminals are also targeting patients' healthcare data, which analysts suggest is now worth more to hackers than their credit card details. The Ponemon Institute think-tank on data protection policy has revealed that cyber-attacks on healthcare providers doubled from 20 per cent to 40 per cent between 2009 and 2013, while the US Federal Bureau of Investigation reported that the personal health information of 4.5 million patients had been stolen in just one such incident.[6] Fake patient identities are created from the stolen data and then used to file false claims for treatment cost reimbursement with insurers, or to purchase medical equipment or drugs that can later be resold for profit. Such developments remind us that while the aggregation of highly sensitive bioinformation provides important opportunities, it also raises significant ethical, regulatory and legal challenges. Many of these pertain to the ways in which this valuable new resource is generated and utilized, including by whom and under what terms and conditions.

How Is Big Data Generated?

'Big data' in this domain is, by definition, an agglomeration of smaller datasets of genetic information, patient records and other health data. Much of this was previously held in large biomedical databases and biobanks, and in the filing systems of hospitals and other healthcare providers. While in some instances – as the Moore and Lacks cases (see Chapter 3) attest – bioinformation was extracted from individuals and reserved for commercial use without consent, the majority of such data was usually acquired through a formal accessioning process undertaken by gatekeepers such as research ethics advisory boards, general practitioners and hospital clinicians. Individuals were formally apprised of the uses to which their data could be put (as dictated by data protection regulations), to which they gave their formal consent. Other individuals agreed to donate on the basis that their tissue and bioinformation would hopefully benefit pure science and wider endeavours to improve healthcare for all of humanity without concerning themselves with the question of how exactly their data might be used and without undergoing any formal consent procedures. This is sometimes described as 'passive data contribution'.

Now, however, other sources of data are emerging. In the field of medical research and healthcare provision, social media is becoming a vital element of big data generation. Two striking characteristics of this kind of data collection are its pervasiveness and its relative invisibility. Millions of people are now contributing bioinformation to an array of online companies, but many remain barely cognizant of this fact. Donations can come in a variety of forms, ranging from data on calorie consumption and stepcount returned via wearable devices and apps, to global fitness corporations such as Under Amour (which hosts MyFitnessPal's 80 million subscribers); to casual reports of unhealthy behaviour such as binge drinking that are uploaded to social media platforms like Facebook as seemingly innocuous status updates; to the raw genetic samples contained in vials of saliva posted directly back to Ancestry.com for genetic analysis. While almost everyone is now contributing bioinformation to such enterprises on a daily basis, relatively few of us are aware of where it goes, how it is used or by whom.

Moves to 'responsibilize' citizens to take greater account of their health and to work actively to improve it have also provided new mechanisms through which to capture this very valuable resource. In fact, many commercial or for-profit genetic research companies now rely on their consumer base to generate the very resource that the company intends to derive profit from selling. 'Prosumption' – the production of digital content by consumers – has become a key source of value in other areas of the informational economy, as evidenced by the huge returns that corporations such as Facebook or YouTube derive from the digital content that their subscribers upload for free. Equally, in the biomedical domain, many patients are now being encouraged, as sociologist Deborah Lupton puts it, to actively employ the digital media technologies used in patient self-care and self-monitoring, 'to digitize themselves: that is, render their bodies into digital form ... to produce data that may be quantified and transmitted to others for their perusal'.[7] 'Prosumers,' those individuals or collectives who contribute genetic data or personal information in this way, have thus become active co-creators of exchange value for the companies or organizations to which they donate.

Examples of these online, company-based digital health platforms include CarePages, Health Unlocked, CureTogether, Smart Patients, Treato and Patient Opinion. Each one invites contributors to upload their own health data and simultaneously access that of other contributors, providing the 'community' with opportunities to share experiences, to compare symptoms and treatment regimes, and to volunteer for clinical trials. By doing this, contributors obtain a greater sense of empowerment and control over their condition. Simultaneously, however, such platforms also link their collective bioinformational and experiential data to massive aggregated datasets (big data) that constitute an exceptional valuable resource for the sponsoring company. In most instances, disclaimers regarding the prospective commercial use of such information are buried deep within the website, leaving contributors unaware that they have effectively relinquished control of their donated bioinformation.

The Potential of Big Data: Hope or Hype?

How and in what ways does 'big data' transform approaches to the analysis of disease and where do the limits of its applications lie? One of the primary ambitions of molecular research in the field of genetics and health over the past 20 years has been to understand and elucidate the relationship between the phenotypical traits of a disease (the way a disease is expressed in an individual) and that individual's genotype (or genetic make-up). The presumption here is that by examining the entire genome of those with particular diseases, it might be possible to identify which sequences of DNA are responsible for that condition. Historically, researchers have focused on trying to identify genetic regions (called candidate sites) in particular individuals that might contain variations (alleles) that could explain their predisposition to disease. The scope of their investigations was, however, limited by the cost of such genotyping, which, in turn, limited sample sizes.

This equation was to dramatically change in the mid-2000s as transformations in genetic sequencing technology revolutionized the scale and speed of analysis. Companies such as Illumina and Affymetrix invented DNA 'chips' that enabled researchers to test for up to 1 million genetic variants at a time. This dramatically reduced the cost of sequencing, driving forwards the development of an entire new research endeavour and an associated economy in what are termed genome-wide association studies (GWAS).[8] Such studies are designed to search the genomes of thousands of individuals for small genetic variations known as single nucleotide polymorphisms, or SNPs (pronounced 'snips') that occur more frequently in people with a particular disease than in people without the disease. What researchers are seeking in the generation and analysis of this 'big data' is *statistically significant* associations between SNPs and particular diseases or traits.

Such projects demand high volumes of data (lots of genomes to examine) but also generate exceptional amounts of data as hundreds or thousands of SNPs and millions of DNA sequences are analysed.

The tremendous potential of this project initially generated considerable excitement in the scientific community, attracting large amounts of investment funding. Leading grant-giving bodies, including the UK's Wellcome Trust and America's NIH, fed millions into GWAS; global consortia, such as International HapMap, were formed to identify common patterns of human DNA sequence variation; and the number of researchers committed to GWAS and to publishing their findings increased exponentially. However, some have argued that it was hype, rather than results, that motivated and sustained this investment. So significant were the potential rewards that researchers began to overstate the strength of the relationship between genetic variation and disease causation, in some instances simply to maintain their funding. Although each genome-wide association study cost around US$10 million or more, the results have been debatable and, many would argue, ultimately disappointing. Although some 2,000 sites on the human genome have proved to be statistically linked with various diseases, in only a very small number of instances did the suspect SNP prove capable of explaining the existence of, or variations in, disease phenotypes. The vast majority of such variants, as some of the harsher critics, such as Jon McCLellan and Mary-Claire King suggest, 'have no established biological relevance to disease or clinical utility for prognosis or treatment'.[9]

The failure to establish strong causal relationships is not a consequence of poor study design but, rather, a reflection of the complexity of disease and interactions between biology and environment. Some 'single gene disorders' such as cystic fibrosis, sickle cell anaemia and Huntington's disease are amenable to this methodology as they are induced by variants in the DNA sequence of a single gene, but most are not. The idea that common diseases such as cancer, heart disease or mental illness could be caused by common genetic variants has been largely disproved by GWAS, for the simple reason that they have produced very few such clear-cut associations. Another reason for the lack of success is because big data analysis typically offers insights into correlations and patterns, but not causes. It can tell us that two things are related, but not why or how. Despite this, the impetus to identify 'genes for' complex disease conditions such as schizophrenia, obesity and Alzheimer's disease remains strong within a Big Pharma industry that has already anticipated the income to be derived from the manufacture of new genetic tests and blockbuster drugs for such conditions. The reach of this particular imaginary is nowhere better evidenced than in the fashion for extending such analyses to investigations of the genetic determinants of other psychosocial traits and behaviours ranging from sexuality to intelligence, economic risk taking or criminality. Two examples are the search for a 'gay gene', and the fenfluramine experiment conducted in New York City in the early 1990s, which sought to find a genetic predisposition for violence in young, male African Americans.[10] While both had begun as fully validated studies, they were later widely discredited and their 'findings' debunked and retracted.

What GWAS have shown is that, while comparisons of case studies and controls can reveal small genetic variations, the effect of these variations is usually very small. Very few of these variations can satisfactorily distinguish those with a particular condition from those without, or provide suitable explanations for the small differences that are evident. By aggregating these small variations into much larger datasets, researchers hope to create algorithms that can pick up on small but possibly significant population-wide variations that could indicate predisposition or shape response to disease and use these to inform diagnosis and clinical treatment. Whether this enterprise will ultimately prove to be successful is at present unknown; however, the hope is that it will usher in a new era of personalized medicine, early diagnosis and preventive interventions. To do this would involve being able to successfully scale the findings down again – to use data on probabilities in populations to inform individual pathways to treatment. The difficulties, and indeed moral and ethical complexities, of employing population-level bioinformation to determine the fate of individuals is a matter to which we return in the final chapter.

The narrative claiming that bioinformation of various different types (DNA sequence information, information on SNPs and other variants, and personal health data in the form of electronic health records) can provide the key to explaining, diagnosing and treating many common diseases has, nevertheless, driven the development of exceptionally robust new industries in gene therapy, pharmacogenomics, stem cell science and regenerative medicine. By 2016, the US NIH was investing more than half of its US$26 billion research budget into these fields of research. The 2,127 per cent increase in publications relating to the genome and genomics that occurred in the 30 years from 1974 to 2014 also gives a sense of the extraordinary depth of investment and the scale of research.[11] The task of translating bioinformational or statistical findings into clinically effective interventions is, however, far from complete. In fact, it has been argued that the continued enthusiasm for gene and stem cell therapies has largely faded in the face of the formidable complexity of the genetic architecture of disease itself.[12] The complexity of biological organisms at the level of cells and tissues is such that, even 60 years after the identification of the gene for sickle cell anaemia, no targeted gene therapy has yet emerged. The prospect of developing successful genetic or cellular-level therapies for more complex conditions remains, inevitably, an even more distant dream.

The transformations in personalized medicine that would purportedly arise with access to electronic health record information are also yet to materialize. As a number of commentators have noted, to generate big data is one thing, but to have the technological capacity, manpower and rights to effectively analyse it is quite another. Difficulties in establishing the interoperability of datasets that may be supplied in incommensurable or even largely unstructured forms can complicate exchange and slow or halt analysis. Inconsistent or inaccurate data, the very significant infrastructural costs of installing and running complex systems for patient records, and the ongoing security and privacy concerns that attend the collection of personal bioinformation have all created further impediments to use. Although by 2016 the US Centres for Medicine and Medicaid Services had paid some US$34 billion in financial incentives to implement electronic health records, in part to facilitate the development of 'personalized' medicine, it remains the case that the most notable improvements in morbidity there have resulted from more conventional public health prevention strategies such as smoking reduction campaigns. Big data has the potential to be a very valuable resource for these endeavours, but only, it seems, if it can be mined effectively.[13]

Predictive Analytics

Despite these difficulties, many believe that 'big data' (in this case, large linked datasets of genetic, health or other bioinformation) can generate an overarching picture of a particular phenomenon, such as predisposition to disease, or even be used to confirm causation, risk or the potential utility of a given intervention. Large datasets have, of course, been used for hundreds of years to reveal population-wide patterns. The census, for example, has been used historically to reveal patterns in mortality – the fact that more people die of influenza in winter, for instance – but it hasn't been possible to 'drill down' into that data to find out anything specific about the individuals that make up the dataset. This is because they are usually anonymized when added. It has, however, become possible to link the very detailed information on health-related behaviour garnered from online platforms and forums with patient records, genetic profiles and large-scale datasets on information such as hospital visitations, to provide a picture of how different kinds of people experience health and disease. By switching between aggregated population-level data and highly personalized bioinformation, researchers can generate models that predict (on the basis of statistical significance) the likelihood of an event occurring. For example, how likely it is that a middle-age woman with a particular genetic profile, who eats a lot of fatty food and takes no exercise, will acquire ovarian cancer.

This kind of predictive analysis of health and disease is now performed by algorithms within computer programs. What is significant about this is the fact that decisions that were once made exclusively by human judgement (such as those determining access to healthcare, likely predisposition to disease or rights to health insurance) are now increasingly performed computationally by software that acts as an autonomous decision-maker. Two recent cases illustrate how ethically problematic this can be. Identifying those at risk of mental illnesses such as depression or alcoholism has always proven complex. Individuals are loath to divulge their risk to healthcare practitioners because they fear wider societal discrimination that might hamper their chances of securing employment or insurance. Psychiatric researchers are now suggesting that one way of getting around this problem of 'non-disclosure' would be to 'mine' online social media posts for information on risky behaviour that might improve the 'detection' of those with serious mental health conditions. The online information, which includes tweets, status updates and images, is, such researchers suggest, more reliable than offline self-reported information, as it 'reflects valid depictions of offline behaviours (e.g., alcohol displays that indicate actual misuse); measures content that is difficult to assess offline (e.g. conversational intensity); achieves previously inconceivable sample sizes; and is more cost effective'.[14]

In a 2016 study, it was revealed that, when asked, over 70 per cent of 1,432 emergency room visitors in the United States consented to a new initiative that would link their social networking site data to their centrally held electronic medical records. Whether their readiness to create a profoundly accurate, although highly invasive, analytical tool arises out of considered reflection or naivety about its prospective use has yet to be established. However, as the authors of the study note, one of the key ethical challenges facing researchers wishing to use social networking data is to ensure that 'vulnerable individuals have a comprehensive and sustained understanding of what participation involves and that consent is monitored throughout the patient journey (i.e., across stages of illness)'.[15] There is also an acknowledgement that making predictions on the basis of disclosures made on social media can be complicated by the fact that such statements may be exaggerated or false and thus lack clinical diagnostic validity.

'Health risk scoring', which arises out of such practices, is, nevertheless, becoming relatively commonplace. This involves, as the name suggests, using computer software to model an individual's likely risk of becoming ill. The use of such models has exploded in the United States since 2007 through the implementation of the 2010 Affordable Care Act's reforms, which compensate insurers on the basis of patient risk. Many questions have been raised about the ethics and the accuracy of making probabilistic assumptions regarding the behaviour of such individuals on the basis of unreliable or partial information. While such predictions may be correct in some instances, the history of actuarial practice reveals that even predictive models looking at much simpler matters – such as life expectancy – have proven to be seriously inaccurate, as demonstrated by the current and associated crisis in pension funding. The attraction of using social media data to inform assessments of risk in the insurance industry was nevertheless demonstrated recently in the United Kingdom when the car insurer Admiral unveiled its new analytic tool for mining individuals' Facebook posts for 'personality traits linked to safe driving', using these to price insurance offerings. Those who write in short, concise sentences, use lists and arrange to meet friends at a set time and place rather than just 'tonight' were identified as conscientious, in contrast to those whose more excitable use of exclamation marks and phrases such as 'always' or 'never' rather than 'maybe', who were determined to be 'overconfident'. Under the scheme, the former were determined to be 'lower risk' and offered discounts of up to £350 on their premiums per year.[16]

Several other concerns surround the application of such models. The first is that they have the tendency to collapse the distinction between correlation and causation. A key aim of big data analysis is to look for correlations or patterns that might suggest general trends of interest. What is lost in terms of specificity at the micro level is said to be compensated for by the wider insights gained at the macro level. The problem, however, is that correlations such as these only tell us *that* a relationship exists; they don't tell us *why*. In other words, they provide no explanation of causation. So, for example, numerous epidemiological studies have revealed that women taking hormone replacement therapy (HRT) also had a lower than average incidence of coronary heart disease, leading many to presume that the HRT was causing the reduction in their risk for this condition. However, later randomized control trials revealed that most of the women had come from higher socio-economic groups and that their lowered risk resulted from better access to healthcare, better diets and better exercise regimes, not from HRT.

Second, big data analysts are often inclined to draw conclusions about the behaviour of individuals and arrive at assessments of their risk through the applied use of these kinds of meta analytics. As Viktor Mayer-Schönberger and Kenneth Cukier put it, 'just as Amazon can use such analytics to recommend books or Google to rank the most pertinent website, so too are they now used in diagnosing illnesses, recommending treatments and even identifying "criminals" before they actually commit a crime'.[17] However, this kind of generalizing, third, facilitates a kind of 'algorithmic branding' of individuals who appear, statistically at least, to meet the criteria for inclusion even if, in reality, the specifics of their case complicate this narrative. For example, a woman known to be carrying a gene for achondroplasia might be characterized as having a very high risk of complications in pregnancy and childbirth (and thus be charged much higher medical insurance premiums), even if she is, in fact, biologically infertile.

Health risk scoring that is performed algorithmically can thus be highly inaccurate and create very serious financial and social hardships for specific individuals who are misidentified as being at high risk. Insurance companies can use such analytics not only to determine the probability that an individual will contract a particular disease or condition, but also what that particular individual could cost to treat. If the sum is too high, that individual may become designated as 'uninsurable'. The ethical implications of allowing some members of society to be abandoned in this way are considerable, and are compounded by the fact that individuals may remain unaware that they have attracted such a negative score until their insurance premiums rise or they are declined treatment or employment. Lack of public awareness about the role of algorithmic techniques, along with the facelessness of the big data industry, combine to obscure where, to whom, or to what, appeals against such decisions could or should be directed.

The Social Implications of Predictive Failures: Biomarkers and Genealogy

Bioinformation has, as we can see, become an absolutely vital resource for new forms of actuarial risk assessment that have profound social and political implications. It can be used to characterize individuals according to their perceived 'riskiness' and to legitimate practices for discriminating against them. Access to drugs or treatments can be limited or curtailed on the basis of what an analysis of their bioinformation suggests the 'likely success rates' of such treatments will be. Personalized medicine is designed to draw on bioinformation about an individual's genetic traits, including the identification of biomarkers that can be predictive of an individual's predisposition to disease or that can suggest their likely response to particular therapies. One of the purported benefits of this is that it would allow interventions to be tailored to suit subgroups of patients sharing similar genetic traits, thus maximizing their effectiveness. We have since seen that such information can be used for less benign and much more discriminatory purposes. These can include denying some individuals access to treatment if they are not considered to have the 'right' bioinformational profile. For example, only those women whose tumours tested positive for the biomarker HER-2 were entered into the pivotal phase III clinical trials for what would become the breakthrough cancer drug Herceptin.

As Monya Baker has argued, what drug and diagnostic companies want more than anything else is 'the ability to predict the future ... rather than waiting years and studying thousands of patients they want to be able to tell who has a disease, which patient will benefit from what drug and whether a drug will have unintended consequences'.[18] The shortcut for delivery of such goals has been the identification of biomarkers from huge extrapolations of genetic and clinical data. Biomarkers are physiological indicators that signal the presence of a disease or condition or the body's response to it. For cancer patients, they might include proteins that are secreted by a tumour, marked biochemical changes in gene expression, or mutations that reflect the body's reaction to the cancer. The protein HER-2 is an example of a successful biomarker as it is overexpressed in about 20–25 per cent of women with breast cancer, those who might best respond to treatment with the drug Herceptin. By using biomarkers, clinicians and drug manufacturers hope to be able to 'shortcut' the process of creating more effective targeted treatments at lower cost and with fewer adverse side effects. However, the biological complexity of many disease conditions, their genetic heterogeneity and the continuing evolution of biological resistance have made the task of identifying biomarkers and translating them into workable clinical diagnostics or interventions so complex that very few have actually emerged. In fact, less than 1 per cent of published cancer biomarkers have actually entered clinical practice.[19] They have, however, performed other kinds of social and political work, acting as powerful instruments for distinguishing between whether or not patients are worth treating, on the basis of their genetic bioinformation and tumour type, or whether drugs should be allowed to be targeted towards specific racial groups (see Chapter 4).

As we have noted above, inherent within the vision for big data is the prospect of personalized medicine, the dream of tailoring an individual's treatment to their unique genetic, phenotypic (and potentially) environmental conditions. In the immediate aftermath of the sequencing of the human genome, scientists emphasized that humans, in fact, shared 99.9 per cent of their genetic make-up and that distinctions between races were statistically insignificant. Nevertheless, some increasingly chose to assert that even a 0.1 per cent difference could affect the way particular racial groups responded to drugs. A watershed moment in the move towards personalized medicine arose when researchers began to target drugs towards specific genetically (and racially) defined populations, as we explored in Chapter 4 through the example of BiDil. Argued by some to be motivated by the hope of intervening 'to maximize the quality of individual and collective life',[20] others believe such practices sediment racial stereotypes and discrimination and echo eugenic beliefs of the past. Nevertheless stratified medicine remains a significant trend, with studies suggesting that the number of US patents for new drugs issued for specific use among designated racial and ethnic groups increased from 0 in 1976 to 29 in 2007, with a further 86 filed between 2006 and 2007 alone.[21] The further accumulation of big data about drug efficacy along racial lines is now actually mandated by the US federal government, which defines the racial and ethnic categories used in both the collection of census data and in biobanking in the United States. The success of racially targeted medicine remains scientifically tenuous, and also potentially dangerous, as it acts to deflect attention away from the underlying social and economic determinants of disease.

Collapse of the Public and Private Domains in the Big Data Economy

All the big data research initiatives outlined above rely for their success on the procurement of large sets of interlinked bioinformation, including genetic sequence data, electronic health records and samples derived from individuals. The big data agenda has fundamentally altered the historical dynamics of collection and exchange in biomedical research. Patients who undergo treatments in hospitals or clinics usually give a formal consent for samples of their tissue, blood or DNA to be taken for diagnostic or research purposes. Most operate under the presumption that their data will be contributed to a study of direct relevance to their condition and thus remain under the custodianship of the clinicians or researchers inviting their participation. As has been noted, patients who are newly diagnosed with a life-threatening condition are particularly vulnerable and are in a 'relationship of dependence' with their care provider.[22] They may consequently agree to participate without being fully cognizant of the implications of their participation. Many remain unaware, for example, that their data may now be added to larger databases for use in a variety of studies to which they have no personal commitment, or which may even work against their personal interests. Inevitably, given the level of corporate interest in this most valuable of commercial resources, some of these prospective users will include pharmaceutical developers and other for-profit companies.

As various scholars have argued, genome sequencing and the digitalization of medical records also pose considerable risks to an individual's data privacy.[23] Tissue samples and paper records sit in one location, but extracted and digitalized sequence data or electronic files become a footloose resource that can be circulated to millions of researchers and company staff working at sites across the globe. One risk attached to this is that 'these hackable digital data could fall into the hands of employers or insurers who may act counter to the interest of the patient'.[24] Another is that this new bioinformational traffic begins to stealthily undermine what has been the relatively secure distinction between research conducted in the public interest and that undertaken for profit. Such outcomes might seem fanciful, but were recently borne out in the case of the UK government's ill-fated 'care data' enterprise.[25]

The UK 'care data' initiative, which was funded by the state, was designed to link together in one centralized database the electronic health records of every individual seen by the NHS. Gargantuan in size, this big data project would, it was argued, provide a resource of unparalleled significance for the advancement of biomedical research and the allied improvement of healthcare. Citizens were called on to 'opt-in' to this sharing economy in the public interest, with senior figures in the medical establishment suggesting that to fail to do so would be irresponsible and 'enormously damaging to the health service'.[26] The programme was scheduled to begin data extraction in spring 2014, but was placed on hold after concerns were raised by the Royal College of General Practitioners, the British Medical Association and Healthwatch England. These included anxieties over the fate of confidential medical data from more than 1 million individuals who had opted *out* of the database. Although they had asked that their bioinformation be removed from the database, it was, in fact, still being shared with third parties because the Health and Social Care Information Centre (HSCIC) had failed to process their requests.

Furthermore, although those who had opted *in* to the programme had been made aware that their data could be used for something vaguely characterized as 'research', many were gravely alarmed to discover that the HSCIC's predecessor unit in the NHS had already sold access to their patient records to the Institute and Faculty of Actuaries, a professional body representing the interests of insurance and investment companies. Although the accessioned data had theoretically been de-identified, it proved possible for those companies to relink it to the individuals from whom it was drawn. This was done by reaggregating critical clinical data from doctors' surgeries with dates of birth and postcodes obtained from searches of other commercial databases. Later investigations revealed that the HSCIC had even developed a costing sheet for providing extracted personal and confidential data for commercial use.[27] This now identifiable bioinformation on medical history was later used for actuarial purposes to 'refine' the prospective cost of critical illness cover for some 47 million UK citizens. Following a review by Dame Fiona Caldicott, the UK's National Data Guardian, the programme was scrapped amid accusations that it had failed to provide clear information or consent procedures for information sharing and had, consequently, thoroughly undermined public trust in the state's ability to protect personal bioinformation.[28]

Conclusion

The aggregation of previously discrete bodies of bioinformation into extremely large relational databases provides unprecedented opportunities to analyse emergent trends and to distinguish 'normal' from anomalous behaviour in a number of research domains, a capacity that also raises serious ethical and regulatory challenges. Although, in principle, big data is primarily concerned with the generation of population-wide trends, it has become evident that the ability to switch between wider aggregations and forms of highly detailed personal data makes the re-identification of individuals and their histories possible at a local level. The concern that electronic databases of medical records or highly sensitive genetic data are being made available to corporate interests without any guarantee that the supplying donors have consented to such uses, or will benefit from them, is raising new political questions and animating fresh approaches to the governance of such materials.

Questions are raised around the use of big data to algorithmically predict the likelihood of an individual developing a particular disease or exhibit certain behaviours deemed detrimental to their health. These predictive analytics mark the increasing use of computer software to make decisions that were once a matter of human judgement, determining access to medical treatment, predispositions to disease or rights to health insurance. The implications of these practices are serious, particularly given the scope for these systems to be highly inaccurate and to create very serious financial and social hardships for specific individuals who are misidentified as being at high risk. Furthermore, on a larger scale, the use of big data to stratify the development and provision of medical treatments along racial, among other, lines raises concerns about the social implications of predictive medicine, and the potential dangers of its ability to deflect attention away from the underlying social and economic determinants of disease.

In response, in part, to the inequalities implicit in the big data agenda, the same information technology that allows the creation of ever larger agglomerations of bioinformation has also facilitated the emergence of new kinds of political advocacy and identity formation. Where once those experiencing particular biomedical conditions might have suffered in isolation, many are now drawing on the power of social media to create connections with others similarly affected. Online platforms and forums generate a space in which new collectives can form. These 'biosocial communities', as anthropologist Paul Rabinow calls them,[29] are bought into existence to share specialized scientific and medical knowledge of their disorder, to combat stigma and to participate in the generation of new and more effective treatments for disease. Many such communities have also sought to wrest back control of 'big data' resources from those who would seek to monopolize them exclusively for their own gain. In developing more egalitarian models of stewardship, they seek acknowledgement as 'co-producers' of interventions and solutions for their conditions, but also as the authors of new, more democratic approaches to genetic resource governance. However, if this principle of an open 'informational commons' is to work, it will be vital to attend carefully to questions of access and governance, and it is to these that we turn in our final chapter.

CHAPTER SIX

Bioinformatic Futures:
The Datafication of Everything?

Introduction

When scientists first began decoding the human genome, they were to spend nearly a decade sequencing its three billion base pairs. Today, a single laboratory can sequence similar quantities of data in just one day. The profound transformations that have arisen in data generation since the early 2000s have revolutionized not only how much can be collected, but also how it can be employed as a productive resource. The rate of growth in sequence data alone has been truly astonishing, rivalling that of the other largest data producers: astronomy, and the social media giants YouTube and Twitter.[1] There are now more than 2,500 high-throughput instruments located in nearly 1,000 sequencing centres in universities, hospitals and other research laboratories in 55 countries around the world. Recent analyses show that the Sequence Read Archive (SRA) maintained by the US NIH National Centre for Biotechnology Information (NIH/NCBI) alone contains more than 3.6 peta-bases of raw sequence data, representing more than 32,000 microbial genomes, 5,000 plant and animal genomes and 250,000 individual human genomes. This, however, represents just a small fraction of all such data, as the majority has not yet been archived. It has been conservatively estimated that, at current rates of growth (a doubling every seven months), one zettabase of sequence data will be generated per year by 2025 (see figure 6.1).[2] Additionally, more than

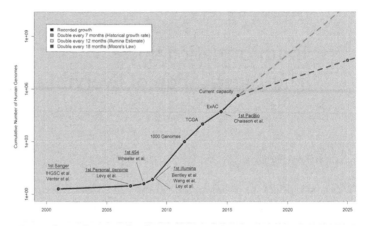

Figure 6.1   The growth of DNA sequencing

Source: http://journals.plos.org/plosbiology/article?id=10.1371/journal.
pbio.1002195#pbio-1002195-g001

100 million and up to 2 billion human genomes could be sequenced by 2025.

Compiling information at this scale provides unprecedented opportunities for meta-level analyses that have the potential to deliver ground-breaking research insights and advanced biomedical breakthroughs. However, the power of this data cannot be realized if it is sequestered in isolated, privately held collections. To be used effectively, it must first be shared and aggregated. The sensitivity of the data and its proven ability to be used in ways that are detrimental to the interests of donors has inevitably raised concerns, leading researchers to acknowledge the need to develop and implement appropriate governance frameworks that build and sustain relations of trust across and between donors and institutions.

Big Data for Whom?

The practice and politics of the 'big data' agenda are, in many respects, paradoxical. Commentators point to the exponential rise in the number of people whose data is available for collection as evidence of the inclusivity of the project. That ever more of us are being swept up as data points in this fashionable project of amassing huge agglomerations of bioinformation is an indisputable fact. The search for associations between bioinformation and an individual's identity, ancestry, health or behaviour has, however, also created norms and practices that exclude, marginalize or exoticize certain individuals or groups in ways that are potentially discriminatory and inequitable. Alternative models are now needed to ensure that this very valuable resource is made available for commercial and other uses in ways that maximize benefits to all. In both the biological and informational sciences, much emphasis has historically been placed on the importance of models of private ownership (such as intellectual property rights) in limiting unlicensed access to bioinformation. Patent rights have subsequently been extended to everything from bacteria to mice on the understanding that exclusivity would facilitate profit-making, despite associated concerns about the anti-commons effect of these kinds of regulation, the embedding of monopolistic practices, the disadvantages of trade secrecy, patent thickets and the like.

Given the concerns over the applications of big data, how should such bioinformation be owned or controlled and who should benefit from its use? One option would be to extend benefit sharing models to encompass all those who have contributed data or information to a given study. Yet benefit sharing models often, as we saw in Chapter 4, prove difficult to operationalize in practice. To whom should benefits be distributed, especially in the genetic realm? Shared genetic make-up implies a shared destiny – does that there-fore translate into shared ownership and shared benefits? The figure of the individual donor implies that just one individual should have rights of ownership and determination over how genetic information can, or should, be used. This is ultimately problematic because genetic material and information don't just pertain to individuals. They are a collective resource of significance to the whole disease community of which that individual is a part.

Benefit sharing models have also been predicated on an assumption that the benefits in question will be largely financial and consist of a percentage distribution of the prof-its flowing from royalties on patented technologies. As the Myriad case (see Chapter 3) demonstrated, patents on genetic sequences such as BRCA-1 and BRCA-2 actually acted to drive up the costs of vital diagnostic test kits and, many argued, also stifled innovation by creating patent thickets that competitors could not breach. The public challenges and contestations that arose in response have triggered a global debate over the ethics of sequestering vital bioinformational resources in privately owned and controlled collections. The alternative, it has been argued, is to free bioinformational data for use as an infra-structural good of unparalleled importance, and to return it to the state of being a 'common' and freely available resource.

The ultimate outcome of the Myriad case reflects many of these changing dynamics. Strong public and legal challenges initiated by the women of the BRCA community eventually succeeded in breaking Myriad's patent stranglehold. On 13 June 2013, in a unanimous decision, the US Supreme Court invalidated Myriad's claims to the isolated BRCA-1 and BRCA-2 genes on the basis that merely isolating genes that are found in nature does not constitute a patentable 'act of invention'. What was perhaps surprising was Myriad's general insouciance about the ruling, an attitude sustained by investor confidence in the company, which, far from slumping after the ruling, in fact reached new stock trading highs. What could possibly explain this outcome? It seems that Myriad, like many other biotech companies, including 23andME, had what has been described as 'an ace up their sleeve'.[3] During its years of supplying and performing patented diagnostic testing in the United States, Myriad had been quietly amassing an immense proprietary database of bioinformation from those undergoing the tests: 'an unparalleled array of data correlating gene mutations with health outcomes and family histories and other phenotypic factors that gave it a unique ability to *interpret* BRCA test results ... an advantage that will long outlive the expiration and invalidation of its remaining patents.'[4] Myriad's decision to monopolize this bioinformation and to leverage it to competitive advantage in the BCRA testing economy invoked a dramatic political response from the breast cancer community, as we shall explore below; but we begin by returning to the idea of a bioinformational commons.

Building a Bioinformational Commons

There has been a growing recognition since the turn of the twenty-first century that the full value of bioinformation can only be realized if it is shared. This is for a curious reason. Bioinformation, like other forms of information, is a peculiar resource in that it is the only one that it is possible to give away, yet still own. Repeated use does not result in its diminution and, as such, it is not subject to the same logic of scarcity that dictates the use values of other material commodities. Hoarding information in such circumstances simply stifles creativity and knowledge production. In fact, as Michael Hardt has argued, 'many such immaterial products only function to their full potential when they are shared in an open way ... not only is it difficult to police exclusive rights over immaterial forms of property but making biopolitical goods private also diminishes their future productivity'.[5]

A range of new modes of resource exchange thus began to emerge in computational science that championed open access to foundational information (such as computer software code) in order to reduce the corporate domination of such resources through the use of patent and copyright. The free and open-source software (FOSS) movement, as it became known, encouraged software developers to 'create a space in which they could develop content and code that could be liberally exchanged and built upon by others'.[6] Several models of resource sharing have emerged in the bioinformational realm that directly mirror these approaches. Each promotes the concept that bioinformational data is a foundational resource that we hold 'in common' and that should be freely available to all. Working on the same principles of 'open-sourcing' or 'sharewaring', donors are asked to contribute genetic material or bioinformatic data for unrestricted use by other members to support collective, but distributed, forms of innovation in the public interest.

Bioinformation, as we know, comes in many forms and works across many registers. So what does a 'bioinformational commons' look like in practice? The following examples might provide some illumination. One of the first such efforts was that undertaken by the Jackson Laboratory in the United States, one of the world's leading centres for the study of mammalian genetics. Jackson performs much of its work on human genetic disorders through the use of genetically engineered mice, known as mouse models. Each mouse is an embodiment of complex sets of manipulated genetic traits and comes with an allied manifest of associated bioinformation on its alterations. In 2009, the Jackson Laboratory began to persuade researchers and those who donated their mouse strains to the facility to make them available as a common resource to other academic researchers (for internal use), free from the usual constraints of material transfer agreements and other restrictions.[7] The aim of this endeavour was to maximize the availability of these valuable resources to the global medical and scientific research community.

Another alternative model for the creation of a bioinformational commons is that exemplified by the BioBricks Foundation.[8] BioBricks is a not-for-profit foundation started in 2004. Its principal function is to create an open resource for sharing genetic sequences and associated bioinformation. The resource is specifically designed for researchers working in the field of synthetic biology, who assemble novel biological entities from a range of different genetic components. The BioBricks foundation operates through the Biobricks Public Agreement (BPA), a legal tool that allows users to share man-made standardized DNA sequences that are known to code for particular functions and that may be linked to particular behaviours or outcomes such as disease. Contributors agree not to assert patent rights over the genetic sequences and knowledge they bank, and users agree to attribute or acknowledge the source of any data they use. In so doing, they together create an open source 'library' of genetic parts and bioinformation that users can freely draw on to advance innovation through collaborative sharing.

Such approaches have greatly facilitated the exchange of genetic and bioinformational resources *within* the scientific community,[9] but they don't address the relationships or agreements (either explicit or implicit) that are made between researchers and members of the general public who donate their information to biobanks. In the following sections, we look to other approaches that seek to take account of the changed relationships between data donors and data users that have been invoked by the big data revolution. These approaches combine aspects of the 'open sourcing' models described above in that they seek to widen access to bioinformational data, but they do so in ways that also enhance donor involvement in determining what knowledge or products are produced and how the subsequent benefits that accrue and are distributed.

Governing a Bioinformational Commons

To better understand how approaches to sharing bioinformation between these parties have evolved, we need to look again at the evolution of biobanks themselves. Early first-generation biobanks (for example, small tissue banks held at local hospitals) were developed out of relations of trust and accountability between researchers and donors who were typically known to one another. Large-scale, second-generation biobanks are less intimate in nature and scale. Donors have no direct or personal contact with either researchers or custodians, and this can complicate or confuse the dynamics of accountability. In such circumstances, those who control the biobank can come to see themselves as the 'owners' of the accessioned material or data, and assume that they have the exclusive right to disperse or dispose of it as they see fit.

So how can we move from a model of ownership towards a bioinformational commons? A new model of custodianship that favours a more collective approach to governance is that of charitable trusteeship.[10] Here, the role of the custodian is conceived as that of 'steward' rather than owner. In this capacity, they are tasked with protecting these valuable resources and conserving the confidentiality and privacy of donors to ensure they are utilized in an ethical way and in accordance with a set of published principles for the biobank's governance. Stewardship signals a new philosophy for biobank governance that promotes and sustains an ethos of bioinformational sharing in the public interest. In this conception, bioinformation and samples are provided as a 'gift' that custodians have an ethical obligation to ensure is held in trust for use by, and for the benefit of, society and the wider biomedical research community. UK Biobank, for example, is a registered charity that makes its resources available to both public and private sector researchers provided their proposed research meets ethical and scientific standards. Their data – including biosamples as well as medical record data and health and lifestyle questionnaires – is donated by research participants on a voluntary basis, with little expectation of direct or personalized feedback on their health.

Such models are also broadening concepts of who or what should constitute a 'custodian'. While responsibility for regulating biobanks has typically rested with an appointed body of scientific and academic experts, moves are now afoot to place donors at the heart of the enterprise in order to assure accountability not just in the use of bioinformational collections, but also in their generation. Patient-led charities have begun to establish their own biobanks to promote research on particular conditions and disorders, such as the UK myalgic encephalomyelitis/chronic fatigue syndrome (ME/CFS) collection, a collaborative venture between the London School of Hygiene and Tropical Medicine, ME charities and private donors and the US NIH.[11] These biobanks are distinctive because they focus on a narrower range of conditions, but also because they actively recruit patient and carer representatives onto the bank's governing body. Many existing biobanks include some lay representatives on their ethics and governance panels (such as lay clergy), but in this case that role is filled by patients and carers who have a direct interest in the research produced by the biobank. They are thus able to directly influence decisions on who may access the resources held by the the bank and the research it supports.

As the UK care data case clearly demonstrated (see Chapter

5), robust and transparent governance of data access is key to maintaining public trust and participation in bioinformational sharing. Custodianship models promote good governance in several ways. First, access is granted on the basis of the scientific merit of the proposed research, its conformance to established ethical principles and consideration of the productive use of the archived specimens or data.[12] Second, the custodianship model democratizes governance by allowing donors to play a strong advisory role in the research approval process. Third, the legal status of charitable trusts creates a much longer timeline of accountability. Unlike commercial ventures, which may go bankrupt, leaving participants faced with the prospect of their donated material being disposed of as 'assets', the trust model ensures such holdings are kept 'in abeyance'. Custodianship therefore resolves issues of conflict and control between stakeholders, including biobanks, researchers, donors and sponsors, recognizing both the altruism of human research participants as well as the need to facilitate broad access to collected bioinformation and the linking of bioinformational collections to advance the public interest in biomedical research. The requirement that charitable trusts be run 'in the public interest' is a useful mechanism for holding biobanks to account. It is in the public interest and, increasingly, community expectations,[13] that donated data be used for the collective benefit of all and that research outputs that could be used against the interests of particular ethnic groups or disease communities (such as those described in Chapter 5) be avoided.

Critics have, however, also noted some drawbacks. First, a charitable trust biobank may be less appealing to venture capital than a privately held resource. The charitable trust model does not exclude collaboration with the private sector, but it promotes access through research partnerships rather than commercial contracts. Second, recognizing obligations to use data 'in the collective interest' does not necessarily translate easily into research practice. Some rights and obligations (for example, the sharing of research data or findings) must be negotiated on a case-by-case basis, others (such as what happens to any leftover human biomaterial) are stipulated in complex and costly to implement access agreements. Third, if payment is made for access to a public biobank, what form should that payment take? Is the aim to generate profits for the bank or to compensate for resource use, in which case how should such dividends be divided and among whom? Or is the charge meant to be analogous to taxes paid for the exploitation of other commonly held resources like oil and gas, in which case should it be returned to public, state-funded institutions such as Britain's NHS?[14] While sharing is a noble value, circulating biobanked materials to researchers outside the host institution (e.g., commercial users) complicates efforts to retain oversight of how such materials are used, to keep donors informed of uses, to ensure they remain 'in the public interest' and to action donor 'opt-out' if they do not.

It is in response to these latter concerns around biobank oversight that the strengths of a different, solidaristic model emerge. This model, developed by Barbara Prainsack and Alena Buyx, reflects the principle that the key motivation to contribute to an endeavour should not be financial but, rather, the 'the willingness of people to support others, reach a common goal or to create some of social value, understood in the broadest sense of the word as something that improves the lives of most citizens'.[15] This, as they argue, involves 'shared practices that reflect a collective commitment to carry "costs" (financial, social, emotional, or otherwise) to assist others'.[16] In contrast to the custodianship model, which views protecting participants from any possible harm as an inviolable responsibility of the data steward, the solidaristic model makes a core assumption that participants are willing to

shoulder certain harms (e.g., the risk of being identified in/
associated with the database and its research by insurers) if
they are outweighed by the collective benefits that their participation could generate. The solidarity model proposes,
therefore, moving towards a system of informed participation that allows donors to express a solidaristic willingness to
accept risks/bear costs in the wider public interest and to sign
a participation agreement to this effect.

This necessarily demands governance structures that
prioritize research with the greatest public health potential
over that directed at profit maximization. Within this model,
research participants and donors are viewed as 'partners in
research to whom the biobank owes respect, transparency and
veracity'.[17] This entails a shift in focus away from risk prevention (especially given that the risks are likely to be small) to
harm mitigation. This could involve, for example, the provision of a compensation fund to provide redress to a person
who does experience discrimination on the basis of their
participation in a biobank. The emphasis placed in this model
on 'communal goods' also helps to diminish any expectations
of individual feedback that might be borne out of biobanking's close association with personalized medicine. Under the
solidaristic model, the communication of research findings
would be collective, through, for example, an online platform,
rather than individualized.

As many critics have noted, the large-scale and future-
oriented nature of biobanks makes it difficult to fully inform
participants of all possible future uses of their data at the
point of donation, a requirement of informed consent.
Informed consent procedures were originally developed to
protect medical research participants from harm by allowing
them to exercise their autonomy. Some argue that the harms
associated with biobank participation are, for the most part,
relatively minor, given that legislation is being introduced

to protect against genetic discrimination and with insurers recognizing that much genetic data has, as yet, failed to offer clear predictors of disease risk. Therefore, we have seen a shift in biobanking towards open-ended or broad models of consent to participate in research. The solidarity model takes this even further, replacing specific consent with veracity or a commitment to truthfulness and accuracy as far as that can be achieved. This might, for example, take the form of a disclosure statement for participants which outlines foreseeable harms and benefits, but which also acknowledges that data may be drawn on in the future for research that cannot yet be envisioned (but which would remain subject to ethical and scientific scrutiny).

The solidaristic approach thus strikes a good balance between overly bureaucratic informed consent procedures which serve the interests of autonomy but can become overly burdensome, and more tokenistic efforts at informed consent designed to tick the ethical boxes needed to facilitate commercial research rather than genuinely encouraging people to reflect on their motivations for participating and the risks this entails. Its particular value lies in its capacity to capture the long-term, altruistic nature of biobank participation, which demands considerable up-front financial investment from operators/funders and personal and emotional investment from donors – with few prospects of immediate returns, despite all the promise of personalized medicine.

Freeing Big Data?

While the custodianship and solidaristic models encourage donors to place information in the hands of a trusted governing body for the common good, an alternative model seeks to position donors as governors of their own data. Until the advent of the big data revolution, such possibilities seemed completely fanciful. The massive data storage and circulation possibilities opened up by the linking together of a ubiquitous pool of on-demand shared computer networks and servers are, however, now making that fantasy a reality. Eric Topol discusses the idea of MOOM (Massive Open Online Medicine), an online cloud where individuals can directly upload their genetic data to improve research and medical outcomes.[18] Although critics have suggested that this vision is unrealistic, we are already seeing cloud data sharing emerging in the health field. Free the Data, a US-based consortium led by Robert Nussbaum at the University of California and managed by Genetic Alliance, is a health advocacy organization that includes policymakers, donors, academic researchers and industry. The aim of this project is to crowdsource the interpretation of the uploaded BRCA-1 and BRCA-2 mutations by putting donors and their data into direct contact with relevant researchers and open access databases. In a campaign of direct action, they began to encourage members of the disease community who were carriers of the BRCA gene to acquire copies of their genetic profiles and test results directly from the laboratories that performed them and to upload them to an online platform of their own making. What makes this initiative distinctive is the website, where donors (patients or those diagnosed with a BRCA-1 or BRCA-2 mutation) are able not only to upload and donate their health information but also to participate in collectively determining to whom that information is made available. Donors become co-producers of the future uses of their bioinformation, able to shape and guide how their bioinformation is used. There are plans to expand the project in the longer term to include those with other health conditions.

Free the Data also constitutes a protest against Myriad Genetics and its legal battle to retain control over knowledge around BRCA-1 and BRCA-2 mutations. As we discussed above, during the period of its patents over the BRCA-1 and BRCA-2 mutations, Myriad amassed a large proprietary database of variants in these genes, allowing it to develop insights into the pathogenicity of specific alleles. Although other tests for BRCA-1 and BRCA-2 mutations are available, those who use Myriad's genetic tests are thus able to acquire a more refined interpretation of their genetic risk. However, Myriad keeps this data private, arguing that this is for reasons of quality control. Critics argue, conversely, that the aim is primarily to allow the company to use the exclusivity of its data as its 'unique selling point' in a crowded but lucrative genetic testing marketplace. As two of the founders of the Free the Data project note:

> [U]nlike the medical literature that is curated for world use and available anywhere – to the immense benefit of patients everywhere – genomic variant data are cloaked in secrecy due to the way some US stakeholders are playing the genetic testing game. If you want your BRCA mutation to be interpreted with the best data available, you have to get both the test and the interpretation performed by a US company in Salt Lake City [Myriad], whether you live in Moscow, Idaho, or Moscow, Russia.[19]

Although this strategy may currently be paying off for companies like Myriad, in the longer term, as initiatives like Free the Data manage to build more robust, extensive and increasingly accurate databases, this kind of hoarding of information will lose its economic purchase. Why pay for something that can be found elsewhere for free? The examples of Myriad and the Free the Data project clearly demonstrate how significant big data governance will be in shaping new markets in bioinformation, but also their potential for ushering in flatter, more nonhierarchical and democratic approaches to the collection and distribution of this vital new resource.

The 'Algorithmically Defined Self': Our Bioinformatic Future?

We began this book by defining bioinformation as a term that refers 'to all information, no matter how constituted, arising from analyses of biological organisms and their behaviour, that can be used to elucidate their structure or function, identify individuals, or differentiate them from each other'. In generating this definition, we focused on information derived from the study of the biology of human beings. But what does the 'study of the biology of human beings' now mean and how is this endeavour being transformed by the big data revolution? Bioinformation for many people means information gained from molecular-level analyses of the genetic make-up of individuals or populations, records of their health status or other associated biomedical data. The big data revolution is, however, rapidly and radically expanding this definition. Whole new datasets of bioinformation are now being generated through analysis of the trillions of pieces of information that we each 'donate' to social media platforms every day. It can be conceived of as biologically derived, as it charts our bodily transit through the spaces and times of our everyday lives: where we go, what we eat, our moods and social behaviour. In this context, distinctions between health data, non-health data and social or other behavioural data begin to dissolve. Each is used to inform the other to create a complex profile of an individual. These profiles are of tremendous interest and value to all those organizations and individuals, whether state, public, private or commercial, who wish to know their 'market' better, including its likes, dislikes, potential or shortcomings.

It is difficult to underestimate the power and the economic value of these new sources of bioinformation. A recent report from the *Washington Post* noted that Facebook now holds on average 98 'data points' on each of its current 1.79 billion subscribers.[20] Extracted from profile descriptions, 'likes' and status updates, these constitute information on an individual's biological and social attributes. These may include, for example, information on ethnicity, expenditure, house purchasing history, political advocacy, mental health, sexuality, general health and even events such as the premature death of siblings. When linked to some of the 10 million publicly available databases that can be mined for further identifiable information, the habits, behaviour and life expectancies of such individuals suddenly become legible, quantifiable and auditable in ways that are historically unprecedented.

Organizations and corporations view these data points as vital new resources, as each can (theoretically at least) act as a proxy that can stand in for complex biological or social experiences. So, for example, repeatedly posted images of seemingly drunken behaviour might indicate that the subject is a heavy drinker and thus a higher car insurance risk. The thesis is that the 'datafication' of everything will allow all manner of human behaviour to be statistically analysed through the use of these kinds of proxy indicators. Large organizations and corporations are drawn to such methodologies as they allow the complexity and chaos of our lived experiences to be reduced to datasets that can be interrogated algorithmically. Computer models determine probabilities of social outcomes, such as the risk that an individual will overspend or engage in unhealthy behaviour, and classify and rank subjects accordingly. Decisions that will dramatically affect all our lives – from being given an expensive new life-saving drug to being allowed to move into better social housing – will increasingly become data-driven. The dream is that this will allow decision-making to become 'cleaner', more impartial, economically efficient and objective. We will become, in effect, *algorithmically defined selves*.

The economic value that can obtain from selling access to

such highly characterized bioinformation is genuinely astonishing. Facebook earned US$3.2 billion from such activities in the third quarter of 2016 alone, a 114 per cent increase in income from the previous year.[21] For some, the ubiquity of bioinformation and the ease with which it can be produced are liberating. Topol argues that smartphones, Fitbits and other biosensing technologies that allow users to collect and interpret data about their health and bodies encourage the 'democratization of medicine', allowing patients to make more informed and independent choices as to the care they need.[22] Others see such technologies are more problematic. Scott Peppet reminds us that this same Fitbit data also provides such 'an incredibly detailed and accurate picture of who you are that it can be used to price insurance premiums and evaluate your credit score', matters that raise serious concerns about data privacy.[23]

Hypercollection and Convergence

In an age when the pervasiveness of big data can only increase, there is perhaps a perception that it is a resource that is too valuable not to be fully utilized.[24] The result is a world in which more and more aspects of our lives are effectively algorithmically defined, one in which the state and other authorities make interventions into our lives (or oblige us to make changes in our lifestyles) based not on who we are, but *on whom our data makes us appear to be*. While this is a longstanding trend (think back to the ways in which social reformers used early statistical data on London to identify areas of poverty and deprivation which they then sought to sanitize), the ability to encode and upload more and more aspects of our lives creates new capabilities – granular-level surveillance of individuals, for example – that are, for many, deeply unnerving. This is particularly so when a picture is

built up on the basis of a reading of accumulated bioinformation that proves to be ultimately inaccurate and thus an unsafe
and unreliable predictor of behaviour. Consider, for example, the single parent denied a mortgage because his or her
data suggests there would be too great a financial risk, or the
retired couple refused health treatment because their chances
of recovery are not statistically good enough. In fantasy world
of *Minority Report*, the Department of Precrime seeks to arrest
individuals before they commit a crime that accumulated
bioinformation predicts they are likely to perpetrate: "I am
placing you under arrest for the future murder of Sarah Marks
and Donald Dublin" – this is a scenario that becomes discon-
certingly plausible. Such eventualities may well come to pass
if we fail to put in place the governance structures necessary
to enable individuals to challenge the false associations and
errors that algorithmic modelling inevitably generates.

Although these dystopic future scenarios seem implau-
sible, the disturbing miscarriages of justice that can arise
from linking together partial or inaccurate profiles of an individual life are perhaps nowhere better illustrated than in our
final example, which takes us back to where we began, with
attempts to identify and arrest those suspected of criminal
behaviour. In 2014, Idaho police investigating a 20-year-old
murder sent a DNA sample to the lab where, using new more
advanced technologies, scientists managed to extract an identifiable sequence of the perpetrator. In this respect, the case
contains echoes of the very first bioinformational techniques
that were used to identify Henry Elliot as the perpetrator of
the 1903 London jewellery theft. Since then, however, we have
witnessed a dramatic scaling up of the enterprise of biometric identification, propelled forwards by the twin drivers of
'hypercollection' and 'convergence'.

Sociologist Barbara Prainsack refers to hypercollection as
the 'darker side of big data'.[25] Technology not only enables

institutions to collect data about their customers and citizens, but has effectively normalized the process to the extent that data is now collected whenever and wherever possible. As she notes, information collected for one purpose may be used for a variety of others neither anticipated nor approved by the original donor. Such was the case in the Idaho investigation. In searching for a match for the crime scene, profile investigators sent the sample not only to numerous police DNA databases, but also to a large private DNA database owned by the Sorenson Corporation, a subsidiary of Ancestry.com. This database consists of samples submitted by the public purely for the purposes of genealogical research. Despite giving assurances that the extracted bioinformation would not be shared beyond the company, police investigators were allowed to run the crime scene sample against the database without either a court order or a warrant. Having identified an individual with a partial DNA match, investigators then data mined the Facebook profiles of his relatives to look for possible suspects. Among them was his son, a filmmaker who had made some documentaries on homicide. The loop apparently closed and he was named as the likely perpetrator. Later tests revealed conclusively that he wasn't, but not before he had undergone a series of gruelling police interviews and been publicly named. His exoneration was indeed lucky, based solely on the fact that the crime scene sample was from a single source and uncontaminated. Had it been otherwise, his fate would have been (wrongly and unjustly) sealed.

The linking of databases in this way creates an unprecedented degree of convergence between information sets, such that it matters less whether the data collected on an individual is itself bioinformation (as defined at the start of this book), and more whether it can be used to *infer* knowledge of a person's health or behaviour. Inferring behaviour from accumulations of big bioinformational data is clearly challenging, and can raise serious concerns around transparency and accountability. While the governance models discussed go some way to providing solutions for those collections easily identified as biobanks, hypercollection and convergence are together creating new registers and architectures of surveillance, the reach of which exceeds anything we have yet experienced. Not only governments, but also public and private actors, are collating and interrogating our bioinformation to produce a 'reading' of us that is increasingly difficult to disavow. Such developments raise questions that we have begun to answer in this book, but which will require much more concerted research and debate to resolve. Who should be allowed to monitor our behaviour or access such data, under what terms and conditions and for what purposes? How can inaccuracies in the analysis of collected bioinformation be remedied? What new decision-makers does the bioinformatics revolution introduce into our lives and how can they be effectively held to account?

Conclusion

Bioinformation has, without a doubt, become one of the key economic and social resources of the twenty-first-century digital revolution, as significant as land was to the agrarian revolution or coal to the industrial revolution. The foundational rules that have shaped the way we understood and sought to govern bioinformation are now being progressively eroded. The increasing volume of traffic between databases and their heightened interoperability renders the distinction between public and private sector collections of bioinformation increasingly obsolete. Donors have historically used such distinctions (between publicly funded and operated biobanks, which they presumed were being run for collective benefit and commercial private sector projects run primarily for profit) to inform their decisions about how to organize their donations. Such distinctions are increasingly hard, if not impossible, to draw. As publicly funded institutions and biobanks are forced to sell access to their collections to sustain their very existence in times of austerity, it becomes all but impossible for the donor to know for certain where or how their donated samples and bioinformation will ultimately be used.

The broader social context within which donors are making those decisions (if indeed they are even actively doing so) has also dramatically changed. While conventional databases such as UK Biobank persist, with their accompanying highly regulated and defined consent protocols, the vast majority of bioinformation is no longer accessioned through such institutions. The ubiquity of social media, with its ability to seduce the public to disclose so much more of their sensitive bioinformation in the virtual world than they would ever dream of offering to mere acquaintances in the real world, is now so pervasive as to have become thoroughly normalized. As a consequence, much of the donation of bioinformation that we engage in every day is now done unwittingly. The need for, and inviolability of, informed consent, which many presumed was a keystone of ethical collecting practice, is crumbling away, eroded by 'tick this box' consent procedures that not only afford zero protection for the donor's privacy, but work to make us all actively complicit in forfeiting our rights to our own bioinformation. Even when consent protocols do exist, few of us bother to read the fine print, meaning that we are unaware, as sociologist Mary Ebeling discovered,[26] of the limitations of the data assurances we are offered. Under the 1996 US Health Insurance Portability and Accountability Act (HIPAA), for example, consent to use your data for marketing or other commercial purposes is no longer needed once it moves beyond the confines of the clinic in which it was first collected. The value of bioinformation as a vital commercial commodity, and the desire to secure it, is, it seems, ushering in a new age in which privacy is no longer a cherished social norm.

While the opportunities that the vast accumulation of bio-information now afford are potentially ground-breaking, there will be no greater challenge in the coming years than that involved in ensuring that the stewardship of this invaluable raw material of the modern age is used justly, fairly and equitably for the collective benefit of all. How can we begin to redress the imbalances created by the contemporary big data climate? Those with the technology and resources can fully capitalize on the hypercollection and convergence of bioinformation, while others who serve as the origin or source of that data find themselves giving up more and more, while simultaneously having less and less say in how that data might be used and to whose benefit. Arguably, the new governance structures and the move to 'free the data' outlined above go some way to addressing these concerns in the context of more traditionally biobanked resources, but are fairly ineffective at addressing the new registers and architectures of surveillance that characterize trade in bioinformation in the twenty-first century.

Consequently, we perhaps find ourselves returning to an idea that we first contemplated over a decade ago. If we cannot all control a resource and how it is exploited, perhaps other mechanisms can be used to ensure that the benefits of exploiting bioinformation are at least more fairly distributed. Inspiration can be found in the way in which these issues are tackled for more traditional resources, like coal, oil and gas, which form the focus of other volumes in this series. Perhaps, as some have suggested, we should consider imposing a tax on the big data industries to ensure that some of the profits of the big data revolution are used to benefit the common good.[27] In this endeavour, the new technologies so valuable in generating big data might also be harnessed to digitally watermark or trace its extraction and exploitation (something not possible in the 1980s bioinformation revolution), allowing us to begin to develop a new system for bioinformation taxation. Perhaps the future of bioinformation lies, after all, not in the development of novel regulatory mechanisms, but, rather, in the novel application of more familiar resource management strategies. While the hope and hype of big data may fail to deliver on all its promises, the potential tax revenue it could generate still has the potential to make a huge contribution to the future of medical research and healthcare. It is to a consideration of how to make such possibilities a reality that a new generation of young researchers and citizen advocates must now turn their minds.

Notes

1   Genesis: What is Bioinformation?

1   *London Daily News*, Tuesday, 17 November 1903, p. 11.
2   *The Standard*, Thursday March 22 1894, p. 7.
3   For a highly accessible introduction to the topic of criminal identification and anthropometry see Cole, S. A. (2009) *Suspect Identities: A History of Fingerprinting and Criminal Identification* (Harvard University Press).
4   See Kay, L. (2000) *Who Wrote the Book of Life? A History of the Genetic Code* (Stanford University Press).
5   For a fuller account of the role of information technology in shaping biomedicine, see Lenoir, T. (1999) 'Shaping Biomedicine as an Information Science', in Bowden, M. E., Hahn, T. B. and Williams, R. V. (eds) *Proceedings of the 1998 Conference on the History and Heritage of Science Information Systems* (ASIS Monograph Series. Information Today, Inc.), pp. 27–45.
6   Wooley, J. and Lin, H. (2005) *Catalyzing Inquiry at the Interface of Computing and Biology* (National Research Council Publication), p. 37.
7   Kitchin, R. (2014) *The Data Revolution: Big Data, Open Data, Data Infrastructures and Their Consequences* (Sage), pp. 2–3.
8   Leonelli, S. (2016) *Data-Centric Biology: A Philosophical Study* (University of Chicago Press), p. 77.
9   Leonelli, *Data-Centric Biology*, p. 77.
10 While we are focusing in this work on human bioinformation and data, it is evident that animal and plant data is also being transformed into a global resource for use in biomedical research as well as wildlife conservation and breeding, agriculture, and the pet trade. For a further discussion of these matters, see Whatmore, S. and Thorne, L. (1998) 'Wild(er)ness:

Reconfiguring geographies of Wildlife', *Transactions of the Institute of British Geographers* 23(4): 435–454; Hayden, C. (2003) *When Nature Goes Public* (Princeton University Press); Greene, S. (2004) 'Indigenous People Incorporated?' *Current Anthropology* 45: 211–237; and Parry, B. (2004) *Trading the Genome* (Columbia University Press).

11 For a fuller description of the various ways in which the tissue was viewed and the impacts this had in social, legal and ethical terms, see Parry, B. (2013) 'The Afterlife of the Slide: Exploring Emotional Attachment to Artefactualised Bodily Traces', *History and Philosophy of the Life Sciences* 35(3): 431–447.

12 Parker, M. and Lucassen, A. M. (2004) 'Genetic Information: A Joint Account?' *British Medical Journal* 329(7458): 165.

13 Cited in Mittelstadt, B. and Floridi, L. (2016) *The Ethics of Biomedical Big Data* (Springer), p. 18.

14 Rose, N. (2009) *The Politics of Life Itself: Biomedicine, Power, and Subjectivity in the Twenty-First Century* (Princeton University Press).

15 Sunder Rajan, K. (2006) *Biocapital: The Constitution of Postgenomic Life* (Duke University Press), p. 114. See also Cooper, M. E. (2011) *Life as Surplus: Biotechnology and Capitalism in the Neoliberal Era* (University of Washington Press). Sunder Rajan and Cooper both combine a Marxist attention to the commodification of 'life itself' – through the creation of global markets in bioinformation, which offer a new way to extract a profitable surplus from the working body – with a Foucaultian emphasis on biopower, or how these knowledges are drawn on by states seeking to technically engineer their population's genetic futures.

16 Lemke, T. (2011) *Biopolitics: An Advanced Introduction* (New York University Press), p. 118.

17 Waldby, C. and Mitchell, R. (2006) *Tissue Economies: Blood, Organs, and Cell Lines in Late Capitalism* (Duke University Press), p. 22.

18 For a more detailed discussion of this process, see Parry, B. (2004) *Trading the Genome: Investigating the Commodification of Bio-Information* (Columbia University Press), ch. 4.

19 Parry, *Trading the Genome*, ch. 7.

2   PROVENANCE: WHERE DOES BIOINFORMATION
    COME FROM?

1 Foucault, M. (1976) *The Birth of the Clinic* (Tavistock
   Publications).
2 John Snow is often seen as the founder of epidemiology for his
   work using data on cholera outbreaks in Soho to track the source
   down to a contaminated water pump. For an interesting overview
   of Snow's work and influence, see McLeod, K. S. (2000) 'Our
   Sense of Snow: The Myth of John Snow in Medical Geography',
   Social Science & Medicine 50: 923–935.
3 Edwin Chadwick was a leading figure in the UK sanitary reform
   movement, who compared birth and death rates in urban and
   rural locations and classes to highlight the health issues of the
   urban poor. See Hanley, J. (2002) 'Edwin Chadwick and the
   Poverty of Statistics', *Medical History* 46(1): 21–40.
4 http://www.ukbiobank.ac.uk.
5 For an overview of the Icelandic Health Sector Database project,
   see Pálsson, G. and Rabinow, P. (1999) 'Iceland: The Case of
   a National Human Genome Project', *Anthropology Today* 15(5):
   14–18; Gulcher, J. and Stefánsson, K. (1999) 'The Icelandic
   Healthcare Database: A Tool to Create Knowledge, a Social
   Debate, and a Bioethical and Privacy Challenge', *Medscape* 1(8):
   6872.
6 Rose, H. (2003) 'The Rise and Fall of UmanGenomics: The
   Model Biotech Company?' *Nature* 425: 123–124.
7 Named after Robert Guthrie, a microbiologist and paediatrician
   at the State University of New York at Buffalo, who developed a
   simple screening test to identify cases of phenylketonuria (PKU)
   in newborns. See Guthrie, R. and Susi, A. (1963) 'A Simple
   Phenylalanine Method for Detecting Phenylketonuria in Large
   Populations of Newborn Infants', *Pediatrics* 32: 338–43.
8 McEwen, J. E. and Reilly, P. R. (1994) 'Stored Guthrie Cards as
   DNA "banks"', *American Journal of Human Genetics* 55(1):
   196–200.
9 Barnes, G., Srivastava, A., Carlin, J. and Francis, I. (2004)
   'Privacy, Safety and Community Health', *Journal of Pediatric Child
   Health* 40: 327.
10 Davey, A., French, D., Dawkins, H. and O'Leary, P. (2005) 'New
   Mothers' Awareness of Newborn Screening, and Their Attitudes

to the Retention and Use of Screening Samples for Research
Purposes', *Genomics, Policy and Society* 1(3): 41–51; Oliver, S.,
Stewart, R., Hargreaves, K. and Dezateux, C. (2005) *The Storage
and Use of Newborn Babies' Blood Spot Cards: A Public Consultation*
(Social Science Research Unit, Institute of Education, University
of London).

11 Hartman D., Benton L., Morenos L., Beyer J., Spiden M. and
Stock A. (2011) 'The Importance of Guthrie Cards and Other
Medical Samples for the Direct Matching of Disaster Victims
Using DNA Profiling', *Forensic Science International* 205(1–3):
59–63.

12 Catalyst (2003) *Guthrie Cards*, at http://www.abc.net.au/catalyst/
stories/s867619.htm.

13 For more critical reviews of deCODE's biobank, see Chadwick, R.
(1999) 'The Icelandic Database: Do Modern Times Need Modern
Sagas?' *British Medical Journal* 319: 441–444; Fortun, M. (2008)
*Promising Genomics: Iceland and deCODE Genetics in a World of
Speculation* (University of California Press); Rose, H. (2001) *The
Commodification of Bioinformation: The Icelandic Health Sector
Database* (Wellcome Trust).

14 Rose, H. (2003), 'The Rise and Fall of UmanGenomics: The
Model Biotech Company?' *Nature* 425: 123–124.

15 Wallace, H. M., Jackson, A. R., Gruber, A. D. and Thibedeau,
A. D. (2014) 'Forensic DNA Databases – Ethical and Legal
Standards: A Global Review', *Egyptian Journal of Forensic Sciences*
4(3): 57–63.

16 Interpol (2008) *Global DNA Profiling Survey*, at www.
interpol.int/content/download/8994/66950/version/2/file/
GlobalDNASurvey.pdf.

17 Interpol (2015) *Fact Sheet: Fingerprints*, at http://www.interpol.
int/INTERPOL-expertise/Forensics/Fingerprints.

18 http://www.virginhealthbank.com.

19 Starr, S. (2015) *What You Think About the 100,000 Genomes
Project*, at http://www.bionews.org.uk/page_515811.asp.

20 Chadwick, R. (1999) 'The Icelandic Database: Do Modern Times
Need Modern sagas?' *British Medical Journal* 319: 441–444.

21 Personal observation at open meeting for UK Biobank
participants, Oxford.

22 Busby, H. (2004) 'Blood Donation for Genetic Research: What
Can We Learn from Donor's Narratives?', in Tutton, R. and

Corrigan, O. (eds) *Genetic databases: Social and ethical issues in the collection and use of DNA* (Routledge), pp. 39–56.

23 See for example Deschênes, M., Cardinal, G., Knoppers, B. M. and Glass, K. C. (2001) 'Human Genetic Research, DNA Banking and Consent: A Question of "Form"?' *Clinical Genetics* 59: 221–239. On the Estonian biobanking project, see Korts, K. (2004) 'Introducing Gene Technology to the Society: Social Implications of the Estonian Genome Project', *Trames* 8: 241–253.

24 For a really interesting discussion of the right 'not to know', see Callon, M. and Rabeharisoa, V. (2004) 'Gino's Lesson on Humanity: Genetics, Mutual Entanglements and the Sociologist's Role', *Economy and Society* 33: 1–27; and Wrexler, N. (1996) *Mapping Fate. A Memoir of Family, Risk, and Genetic Research* (University of California Press).

25 Korts, K. (2004) 'Introducing Gene Technology to the Society: Social Implications of the Estonian Genome Project', *Trames* 8: 241–253.

26 See Greenhough, B. (2006) 'Decontextualised? Dissociated? Detached? Mapping the Networks of Bioinformatics Exchange', *Environment and Planning A* 38(3): 445–463.

27 Barnes, G., Srivastava, A., Carlin, J. and Francis, I. (2004) 'Privacy, Safety and Community Health', *Journal of Pediatric Child Health* 40: 327.

28 Duncan, R. (2004) 'Respecting the Autonomy of Patients', *Journal of Paediatric Child Health* 40: 326; Genetic Health Services Victoria (2003) *Guthrie Cards*, at www.genetichealthvic.net.au/pages/diagnosis/guthriecards.html; Laberge, C., Kharaboyan, L. and Avard, D. (2004) 'Newborn Screening, Banking and Consent', at http://www.humgen.org/int/GE/en/2004-3.pdf; Spriggs, M. (2004) 'Defending De-identification of Research Samples on the Grounds of Public Health Benefit', *Journal of Paediatric Child Health* 40: 327–328.

29 Deschênes, M., Cardinal, G., Knoppers, B. M. and Glass, K. C. (2001) 'Human Genetic Research, DNA Banking and Consent: A Question of "Form"?' *Clinical Genetics* 59: 221–239.

30 World Medical Assembly (1964) *Helsinki Declaration*, Article 22.

31 For a useful discussion of the issues around informed consent, see Kaye, J. (2004) 'Abandoning Informed Consent: The Case of Genetic Research in Population Collections', in Tutton, R. and

Corrigan, O. (eds) *Genetic Databases: Social and Ethical Issues in the Collection and Use of DNA* (Routledge), pp. 117–138.

32 We return to these issues in Chapter 6 when we explore how bioinformation may be governed in the future, including considering the role of donors in deciding how their data could and should be used.

33 See Corrigan, O. (2004) 'Informed Consent: The Contradictory Ethical Safeguards in Pharmacogenomics', in Tutton, R. and Corrigan, O. (eds) *Genetic Databases: Social and Ethical Issues in the Collection and Use of DNA* (Routledge), pp. 78–97; Hoeyer, K. (2003) '"Science Is Really Needed – That's All I Know": Informed Consent and the Non-Verbal Practices of Collecting Blood for Genetic Research in Northern Sweden', *New Genetics and Society* 22(3): 229–244.

34 Nuffield Council on Bioethics (2008) *The Forensic Use of Bioinformation: Ethical Issues*, at http://nuffieldbioethics.org/wp-content/uploads/The-forensic-use-of-bioinformation-ethical-issues.pdf.

35 Kowal, E. (2013) 'Orphan DNA: Indigenous Samples, Ethical Biovalue and Postcolonial Science', *Social Studies of Science* 43(4): 577–597.

36 This is highlighted by the anthropological work of scholars such as Adriana Petryna, whose ethnographic research on the outsourcing of clinical trials from the United Kingdom and the United States to places such as Poland found that the value of the bioinformation extracted from these trials is seen as being enhanced where participants with high levels of education and literacy are reckoned to be capable of giving 'meaningful' informed consent. See Petryna, A. (2007) 'Clinical Trials Offshored: On Private Sector Science and Public Health', *BioSocieties* 2: 21–40; and Petryna, A. (2009) *When Experiments Travel: Clinical Trials and the Global Search for Human Subjects* (Princeton University Press).

37 Andersen, B. and Zoëga, T. (1999) 'Letter/Icelandic Genetics', *Nature Biotechnology* 17: 517.

38 For an excellent critical overview of the Human Genome Diversity Project, see M'charek, A. (2005) *The Human Genome Diversity Project: An Ethnography of Scientific Practice* (Cambridge University Press).

39 Cavalli-Sforza, L. L. (2005) 'The Human Genome Diversity

Project: Past, Present and Future', *Nature Reviews Genetics* 6:
333–340.

40 Reardon, J. and TallBear, K. (2012) '"Your DNA Is Our History":
Genomics, Anthropology, and the Construction of Whiteness as
Property', *Current Anthropology* 53(S5): S233–S245.

41 M'charek, A. (2014) 'Race, Time and Folded Objects: The HeLa
Error', *Theory, Culture and Society* 31(6): 29–56.

3   PROPERTY: WHO OWNS BIOINFORMATION?

1 For an insight into the Human Genome Project and the social
and scientific concerns of the time, see Kevles, D. J. and Hood,
L. (1993) *Code of Codes: Scientific and Social Issues in the Human
Genome Project* (Harvard University Press).

2 The International Human Genome Sequencing Consortium
included: (1) The Whitehead Institute/MIT Center for Genome
Research, Cambridge, MA, USA; (2) The Wellcome Trust Sanger
Institute, The Wellcome Trust Genome Campus, Hinxton,
Cambridgeshire, UK; (3) Washington University School of
Medicine Genome Sequencing Center, St. Louis, MO, USA; (4)
US DOE Joint Genome Institute, Walnut Creek, CA, US; (5)
Baylor College of Medicine Human Genome Sequencing Center,
Department of Molecular and Human Genetics, Houston,
TX, USA; (6) RIKEN Genomic Sciences Center, Yokohama,
Japan; (7) Genoscope and CNRS UMR-8030, Evry, France; (8)
GTC Sequencing Center, Genome Therapeutics Corporation,
Waltham, MA, USA; (9) Department of Genome Analysis,
Institute of Molecular Biotechnology, Jena, Germany; (10)
Beijing Genomics Institute/Human Genome Center, Institute
of Genetics, Chinese Academy of Sciences, Beijing, China; (11)
Multimegabase Sequencing Center, The Institute for Systems
Biology, Seattle, WA, USA; (12) Stanford Genome Technology
Center, Stanford, CA, USA; (13) Stanford Human Genome
Center and Department of Genetics, Stanford University School
of Medicine, Stanford, CA, USA; (14) University of Washington
Genome Center, Seattle, WA, USA (15) Department of Molecular
Biology, Keio University School of Medicine, Tokyo, Japan; (16)
University of Texas Southwestern Medical Center at Dallas,
Dallas, TX, USA; (17) University of Oklahoma's Advanced Center

for Genome Technology, Dept. of Chemistry and Biochemistry, University of Oklahoma, Norman, OK, USA; (18) Max Planck Institute for Molecular Genetics, Berlin, Germany; (19) Cold Spring Harbor Laboratory, Lita Annenberg Hazen Genome Center, Cold Spring Harbor, NYU, USA; (20) GBF – German Research Centre for Biotechnology, Braunschweig, Germany.

3 National Human Genome Research Institute (2016), at https://www.genome.gov/12011238/an-overview-of-the-human-genome-project/.

4 National Human Genome Research Institute (2012), at https://www.genome.gov/10001792/largescale-sequencing-goals/.

5 Kant, I. (1993) *Grounding for the Metaphysics of Morals: On a Supposed Right to Lie Because of Philanthropic Concerns*, 3rd ed. (Hackett), p. 36.

6 Hickey, R. (2012) 'Seeking to Understand the Definition of Slavery', in Allain, J. (ed.) *The Legal Understanding of Slavery: From the historical to the contemporary* (Oxford University Press), pp. 220–241.

7 Radin, M. J. (1996) *Contested Commodities: The Trouble with Trade in Sex, Children, Body Parts and Other Things* (Harvard University Press), p. 58.

8 Landecker, H. (2010) *Culturing Life: How Cells Became Technologies* (Harvard University Press).

9 Tully, J. (1982) *A Discourse on Property: John Locke and His Adversaries* (Cambridge University Press).

10 For a fuller explication of the details of this case and its implications, see Parry, B. (1994) *Trading the Genome: The Commodification of Bioinformation* (Columbia University Press).

11 *Diamond v. Chakrabarty* (1980) 447 U.S. 303, p. 320.

12 For more on the Moore case, see Waldby, C. and Mitchell, R. (2006) *Tissue Economies: Blood, Organs, and Cell Lines in Late Capitalism* (Duke University Press), pp. 88–109.

13 Skloot, R. (2010) *The Immortal Life of Henrietta Lacks* (New York: Crown Publishing Group).

14 For more on the Hagahai patent case, see Kirsh, S. (2004) 'Property Limits: Debates on the Body in Nature and Culture', in Hirsch, E. and Strathern, M. (eds) *Transactions and Creations: Property Debates and the Stimulus of Melanesia* (Oxford: Bergahan), pp. 21–39.

15 Widdows, H. (2013) *The Connected Self: Ethics and Governance of the Genetic Individual* (Cambridge University Press).

16 See also Shiva, V. (2004) 'TRIPS, Human Rights and the Public Domain', *Journal of World Intellectual Property* 7: 597–760.

17 The European Patent Convention states in Article 52 that 'biotechnological inventions shall be patentable if they concern biological material which is isolated from its natural environment or produced by any means of a technical process even if it previously existed in nature'; cited at https://www.droit-technologie.org/actualites/the-directive-9844-ec-for-the-legal-protection-of-biotechnological-inventions-a-commentary-of-its-articles/.

18 The European Patent Convention (2008) Article 52 (Rule 29), at https://www.epo.org/law-practice/legal-texts/html/epc/2016/e/r29.html.

19 Baldwin, A. L. and Cook-Deegan, R. (2013) 'Constructing Narratives of Heroism and Villainy: Case Study of Myriad's BRACAnalysis® Compared to Genentech's Herceptin®'. *Genome Medicine* 5(8): p. 9.

20 Baldwin and Cook-Deegan, 'Constructing Narratives of Heroism and Villainy', p. 9.

4   MARKETS: WHO CONSUMES BIOINFORMATION?

1 http://www.independent.co.uk/life-style/health-and-families/health-news/the-angelina-jolie-effect-her-mastectomy-revelation-doubled-nhs-breast-cancer-testing-referrals-9742074.html.

2 http://www.mcrc.manchester.ac.uk/our-research/biobank.

3 http://www.nature.com/scitable/topicpage/huntington-s-disease-the-discovery-of-the-851.

4 Wexler, A. (1996) *Mapping Fate: A Memoir of Family, Risk and Genetic Research* (University of California Press).

5 http://www.ukbiobank.ac.uk/about-biobank-uk/.

6 http://www.nature.com/news/technology-the-1-000-genome-1.14901.

7 Paul, S. M., Mytelka, D. S., Dunwiddie, C. T., Persinger, C. C., Munos, B. H., Lindborg, S. R., and Schacht A. L. (2010) 'How to Improve R&D Productivity: The Pharmaceutical Industry's Grand Challenge', *Nature Reviews Drug Discovery* 9(3): 203–214.

8 For an examination of the impact of pharmacogenomics on clinical practice, see Hedgecoe, A. M. (2006) 'Context, Ethics and Pharmacogenetics', *Studies in History and Philosophy of Science, Part C: Studies in History and Philosophy of Biological and Biomedical Sciences* 37(3): 566–582.

9 Cohn, J. N., Johnson, G., Ziesche, S., Cobb, F., Francis, G., Tristani, F., Smith, R., Dunkman, W. B., Loeb, H. and Wong, M. (1991) 'A Comparison of Enalapril with Hydralazine-Isosorbide Dinitrate in the Treatment of Chronic Congestive Heart Failure', *New England Journal of Medicine* 325(5): 303–310.

10 Carson, P., Ziesche, S., Johnson, G. and Cohn, J. N. (1999) 'Racial Differences in Response to Therapy for Heart Failure: Analysis of the Vasodilator-Heart Failure Trials. Vasodilator-Heart Failure Trial Study Group', *Journal Cardiac Failure* 5(3): 178–187.

11 Taylor, A. L., Ziesche, S., Yancy, C., Carson, P., D'Agostino, R., Jr, Ferdinand, K., Taylor, M., Adams, K., Sabolinski, M., Worcel, M., Cohn, J. N. and African American Heart Failure Trial Investigators (2004) 'Combination of Isosorbide Dinitrate and Hydralazine in Blacks with Heart Failure', *New England Journal Medicine* 351(20): 2049–2057.

12 Nelson, N., Keating, P. and Cambrosio, A. (2013) 'On being "Actionable": Clinical Sequencing and the Emerging Contours of a Regime of Genomic Medicine in Oncology', *New Genetics & Society* 32: 405–428.

13 NIH (no date) 'What is the HapMap', at https://hapmap.ncbi.nlm.nih.gov/whatishapmap.html. Note that the HapMap literature is keen to stress that the object of this exercise is not to find links between genetic variants and diseases, but to link genetic variants to risk factors for developing disease.

14 M'charek, A. (2008) 'Silent witness, Articulate Collective: DNA Evidence and the Inference of Visible Traits', *Bioethics* 22(9): 519–528.

15 Nuffield Council on Bioethics (2008) *The Forensic Use of Bioinformation: Ethical Issues*, at http://nuffieldbioethics.org/wp-content/uploads/The-forensic-use-of-bioinformation-ethical-issues.pdf.

16 https://mediacenter.23andme.com/en-eu/blog/2015/10/14/23andme-raises-115-million-in-series-e-financing-led-by-fidelity-management-research-company/.

17 http://www.bioworld.com/content/dna-forensics.

18 Ebeling, M. F. E. (2016) *Healthcare and Big Data: Digital Spectres and Phantom Objects* (Palgrave MacMillan).

19 See the essays in part one of Parry, B., Greenhough, B., Dyck, I. and Brown, T. (2015) *Bodies Across Borders: The Global Circulation of Body Parts, Medical Tourists and Professionals* (Ashgate).

20 FAO (1983), at http://www.fao.org/docrep/x5563e/X5563e0a.htm.

21 Hardin, G. (1968) 'The Tragedy of the Commons', *Science* 162(3859): 1243–1248.

22 https://www.cbd.int.

23 Lock, M. (2003) 'The Alienation of Body Tissues and the Biopolitics of Immortalised Cell Lines', in Scheper-Hughes, N. and Wacquant, L. (eds) *Commodifying Bodies* (Sage), p. 51.

24 Chadwick, R. and Berg, K. (2001) 'Solidarity and Equity: New Ethical Frameworks for genetic Databases', *Nature Reviews Genetics* 2(4): 318–321.

25 Simm, K. (2005) 'Benefit-Sharing: An Inquiry Regarding the Meaning and Limits of the Concept in Human Genetic Research', *Genomics, Society and Policy* 1(2): pp. 29–40.

26 For more on benefit sharing, see Knoppers, B. M. (2000) 'Population Genetics and Benefit Sharing', *Community Genetics* 3(4): 212–214; Hayden, C. (2003) *When Nature Goes Public: The Making and Unmaking of Bioprospecting in Mexico* (Princeton University Press); Parry, B. (2004) *Trading the Genome* (Columbia University Press).

27 Rabinow, P. (1999) *French DNA: Trouble in Purgatory* (University of Chicago Press).

28 Haddow, G., Cunningham-Burley, S., Bruce, A. and Parry, S. (2004) 'Generation Scotland Primary Consultation Exercise 2003–04: Public and Stakeholder Views from Focus Groups and Interviews', INNOGEN Working Paper, no. 20 (ESRC).

29 For a discussion of how genetic data shapes patient's interactions with medical practitioners, see Nelkin, D. (1993) 'The Social Power of Genetic Information', in Kevles, D. and Hood, L. (eds) *The Code of Codes: Scientific and Social Issues in the Human Genome Project* (Harvard University Press), pp. 177–190; and Hall, E. (2004) 'Spaces and Networks of Genetic Knowledge Making: The "Geneticization" of Heart Disease', *Health and Place* 10: 311–318.

30 Progress Educational Trust, at http://www.bionews.org.uk/page_515811.asp.
31 Hamilton, D. P. (2008) 'deCODEme's underwhelming personal-genomics service', at http://venturebeat.com/2008/01/23/decodemes-maddening-and-underwhelming-personal-genomics-service.
32 Nelson, Keating and Cambrosio contrast this kind of 'predictive' data about genetic risk with the more 'actionable' data now being generated by tumour sequencing. In contrast to the kind of predictive testing used to identify BRCA-1 and BRCA-2 mutations, tumour sequencing is used to identify which treatments might be most effective, a move that might be described as taking bioinformation from bench (or the research context) to bedside, enabling the 'smart' use of particular drug therapies tailored towards molecular mutations; see Nelson, N., Keating, P. and Cambrosio, A. (2013) 'On Being "Actionable": Clinical Sequencing and the Emerging Contours of a Regime of Genomic Medicine in Oncology', New Genetics & Society 32: 405–428 (p. 411).
33 Styrkarsdottir, U., Thorleifsson, G., Sulem, P., Gudbjartsson, D. F., Sigurdsson, A., Jonasdottir, A. ... and Stefansson K. (2013) 'Nonsense Mutation in the LGR4 Gene is Associated with Several Human Diseases and Other Traits', Nature 497(7450): 517–520.
34 Fortun, M. (2008) Promising Genomics: Iceland and deCODE Genetics in a World of Speculation (University of California Press).
35 Interview by Greenhough, April 2001.
36 Sunder Rajan, K. (2006) Biocaptial: The Constitution of Postgenomic Life (Duke University Press).
37 Kowal, E. (2013) 'Orphan DNA: Indigenous Samples, Ethical Biovalue and Postcolonial Science', Social Studies of Science 43(4): 577–597.
38 Reardon, J. and TallBear, K. (2012) '"Your DNA Is Our History": Genomics, Anthropology, and the Construction of Whiteness as Property', Current Anthropology 53(S5): S233–S245.
39 Kowal, E. (2013) 'Orphan DNA: Indigenous Samples, Ethical Biovalue and Postcolonial Science', Social Studies of Science 43(4): 577–597; and Reardon, J. and TallBear, K. (2012) '"Your DNA Is Our History": Genomics, Anthropology, and the Construction of Whiteness as Property', Current Anthropology 53(S5): S233–S245.

5 THE BIG DATA REVOLUTION

1 The US Centers for Medicare and Medicaid Services, at https://www.cms.gov/research-statistics-data-and-systems/statistics-trends-and-reports/nationalhealthexpenddata/nhe-fact-sheet.html.

2 Wesolowski, A., Buckee, C. O., Bengtsson, L., Wetter, E., Xin, L. and Tatem, A. J. (2014) 'Commentary: Containing the Ebola Outbreak – The Potential and Challenge of Mobile Network Data', *PLOS Currents* 6: 1–17.

3 Broniatowski, D. A., Paul, M. J., and Dredze, M. (2013) 'National and Local Influenza Surveillance through Twitter: An Analysis of the 2012–2013 Influenza Epidemic', *PLOS One* 8(12): 1–8.

4 US Department for Health and Human Services (2016) *HHS FY2016 Budget in Brief*, at https://www.hhs.gov/about/budget/budget-in-brief/nih/index.html.

5 Accenture (2014) *What's Holding Up EMR Adoption? How Europe's Public Hospitals Will Redefine Healthcare by 2030*, at https://www.accenture.com/us-en/insight-getting-emr-back-fast-lane-summary.

6 Humer, C. and Finkle, J. (2014) *Your Medical Record Is Worth More to Hackers Than Your Credit Card*, at http://www.reuters.com/article/us-cybersecurity-hospitals-idUSKCN0HJ21I20140924.

7 Lupton, D. (2014) 'The Commodification of Patient Opinion: The Digital Patient Experience Economy in the Age of Big Data', *Sociology of Health and Illness* 36(6): 856–869 (p. 857).

8 National Human Genome Research Institute (2015) *Genome-Wide Association Studies*, at https://www.genome.gov/20019523/.

9 McClellan, J. and King, M. C. (2010) 'Genetic heterogeneity in human disease', *Cell* 141(2): 210–217 (p. 213).

10 Inda, J. X. and Merz, S. (2015) *Questioning Racial Prescriptions: An Interview with Jonathan Xavier Inda*, at http://www.theoryculturesociety.org/interview-with-jonathan-xavier-inda-on-racial-prescriptions/.

11 Joyner, M. J., Paneth, N., and Ioannidis, J. P. A. (2013) 'What Happens When Underperforming Big Ideas in Research Become Entrenched?' *JAMA* 316(13): 1355–1356.

12 Joyner, Paneth and Ioannidis, 'What Happens When Underperforming Big Ideas in Research Become Entrenched?'

13 Joyner, Paneth and Ioannidis, 'What Happens When Underperforming Big Ideas in Research Become Entrenched?'

14 Inkster, B., Stillwell, D., Kosinski, M., and Jones, P. (2016) 'A Decade into Facebook: Where Is Psychiatry in the Digital Age?' *The Lancet* 3(11): 1087.

15 Inkster, Stillwell, Kosinski and Jones, 'A Decade into Facebook', p. 1089.

16 Ruddick, G. (2016) 'Admiral to Price Car Insurance Based on Facebook Posts', at https://www.theguardian.com/technology/2016/nov/02/admiral-to-price-car-insurance-based-on-facebook-posts.

17 Mayer-Schönberger, V. and Cukier, K. (2013) *Big Data: A Revolution That Will Transform How We Live, Work and Think* (John Murray), p. 12.

18 Baker, M. (2005) 'In Biomarkers We Trust?' *Nature Biotechnology* 23(3): 297–304 (p. 297).

19 Kern, S. E. (2012) 'Why Your New Cancer Biomarker May Never Work: Recurrent Patterns and Remarkable Diversity in Biomarker Failures', *Cancer Research* 72(23): 6091–6101.

20 Inda, J. X. and Merz, S. (2015) *Questioning Racial Prescriptions: An Interview with Jonathan Xavier Inda*, at http://www.theoryculturesociety.org/interview-with-jonathan-xavier-inda-on-racial-prescriptions/.

21 Kahn, J. (2013) *Race in a Bottle: The Story of BiDil and Racialized Medicine in a Post-Genomic Age* (Columbia University Press).

22 Blanchard, J., Nayar, S. and Lurie, N. (2007) 'Patient–Provider and Patient–Staff Racial Concordance and Perceptions of Mistreatment in the Health Care Setting', *Journal of General Internal Medicine* 22(8): 1184–1189.

23 Hoeyer, K. (2008) 'The Ethics of Research Biobanking: A Critical Review of the Literature', *Biotechnology and Genetic Engineering Reviews* 25: 429–452; Parry, B. (2005) 'From the Corporeal to the Informational: Exploring the Scope of Benefit Sharing Agreements and their Applicability to Sequence Databases', in Theile, F. and Ashcroft, R. E. (eds) *Bioethics in a Small World* (Springer), pp. 73–91.

24 Blanchard, J., Nayar, S. and Lurie, N. (2007) 'Patient–Provider and Patient–Staff Racial Concordance and Perceptions of Mistreatment in the Health Care Setting', *Journal of General Internal Medicine* 22(8): 1184–1189.

25 Health and Social Information Service (UK) (2014) *Care.data*, at http://www.hscic.gov.uk/gpes/caredata.
26 Knapton, S. (2016) 'How the NHS Got It So Wrong with care.data', *Telegraph*, 7 July, at http://www.telegraph.co.uk/science/2016/07/07/how-the-nhs-got-it-so-wrong-with-caredata/. See also Presser, L., Hruskova, M., Rowbottom, H. and Kancir, J. (2015) *Care.data and Access to UK Health Records: Patient Privacy and Public Trust*, at http://techscience.org/a/2015081103/.
27 Ramesh, R. (2013) *£140 Could Buy Private Firms Data on NHS Patients*, at https://www.theguardian.com/technology/2013/may/17/private-firms-data-hospital-patients.
28 Several studies and reports offer useful insights into the social and economic implications of this scandal; see, e.g., http://techscience.org/a/2015081103); https://www.gov.uk/government/uploads/system/uploads/attachment_data/file/535024/data-security-review.PDF; https://you.38degrees.org.uk/petitions/stop-selling-our-nhs-records-to-private-companies-1; https://www.theguardian.com/technology/2013/may/17/private-firms-data-hospital-patients; https://actions.sumofus.org/a/scrap-the-sale-of-our-medical-records.
29 Rabinow, P. (1996) 'Artificiality and Enlightenment: From Sociobiology to Biosociality', in Rabinow, P. (ed.) *Essays on the Anthropology of Reason* (Princeton University Press), pp. 91–111.

6   Bioinformatic Futures: The Datafication of Everything?

1   Mayer-Schönberger, V. and Cukier, K. (2013) *Big Data: A Revolution That Will Transform How We Live, Work and Think* (John Murray).
2   Stephens, Z. D., Lee, S. Y., Faghri, F., Campbell, R. H., Zhai, C., Efron, M. J. ... and Robinson, G. E. (2015) 'Big Data: Astronomical or Genomical?', *PLoS Biology* 13(7): e1002195. DOI:10.1371/journal.pbio.1002195.
3   Conley, J. M., Cook-Deegan, R. and Lázaro-Muño, G. (2014) 'Myriad after Myriad: The Proprietary Data Dilemma', *North Carolina Journal of Law and Technology* 15(4): 597–637 (p. 600).
4   Conley, Cook-Deegan and Lázaro-Muño, 'Myriad after Myriad'.

5 Hardt, M. (2010) 'Two Faces of the Apocalypse', *Polygraph* 22: 265–274 (p. 268).
6 Kloppenburg, J. (2010) 'Impeding Dispossession, Enabling Repossession: Biological Open Source and the Recovery of Seed Sovereignty', *Journal of Agrarian Change* 10(3): 367–388.
7 Einhorn, D. and Heimes, R. (2009) 'Creating a Mouse Academic Research Commons', *Nature Biotechnology* 27: 890–891.
8 www.biobricks.org.
9 It is worth noting that in other fields of biological research, notably ecology, questions remain about the usefulness and feasibility of data sharing initiatives. Critics highlight the ways in which data sharing within scientific communities is limited by a lack of appropriate infrastructures, and by existing practices of data collection (which may render datasets incompatible with potential collaborators' projects and systems). Baker and Millerand suggest that data provenance may also play a key role in addressing these limitations, by sharing alongside bioinformation a history of how that data was produced, cleaned and manipulated. Hine further highlights the limitations of bioinformation for performing particular kinds of research. Her interviews with biologists suggested that bioinformation was a poor proxy for more 'hands-on' engagements with specimens in the lab or field. See Baker, K. S. and Millerand, F. (2010) 'Infrastructuring Ecology: Challenges in Achieving Data Sharing', in Parker, J. N., Vermulen, N. and Penders, B. (eds) *Collaboration in the New Life Sciences* (Ashgate), pp. 111–138; Hine, C. (2013) 'The Emergent Qualities of Digital Specimens in Biology', *Information, Communication & Society* 16(7): 1157–1175.
10 Winickoff, D. and Winickoff, R. (2003) 'The Charitable Trust as a Model for Genomic Biobanks', *New England Journal of Medicine* 349(12): 1180–1184.
11 http://www.meresearch.org.uk/our-research/completed-studies/biobank/.
12 Yassin, R., Lockhart, N., González del Riego, M., Pitt, K., Thomas, J. W., Weiss, L. and Compton, C. (2010) 'Custodianship as an Ethical Framework for Biospecimen-Based Research', *Cancer Epidemiology, Biomarkers & Prevention* 19(4): 1012–1015.
13 Stewart, C., Aparicio, L., Lipworth, W. and Kerridge, I. (2014) 'Public Umbilical Cord Blood Banking and Charitable Trusts', in Goold, I., Greasley, K., Herring, J. and Skene, L. (eds) *Persons,*

Parts and Property: How Should we Regulate Human Tissue in the 21st Century (Hart), pp. 53–66.

14 Verlinden, M., Nys, H., Ectors, N. and Huys, I. (2016) 'Qualitative Study on Custodianship of Human Biological Material and Data Stored in Biobanks', *BMC Medical Ethics* 17(15); DOI:10.1186/s12910-016-0098-0.

15 Prainsack, B. and Buyx, A. (2017) *Solidarity in Biomedicine and Beyond* (Cambridge University Press), p. 4.

16 Prainsack, B. and Buyx, A. (2012) 'Solidarity in Contemporary Bioethics – Towards a New Approach', *Bioethics* 26(7): 343–350 (p. 346).

17 Prainsack, B. and Buyx, A. (2011) *Solidarity: Reflections on an Emerging Concept in Bioethics*, at http://nuffieldbioethics.org/wp-content/uploads/2014/07/Solidarity_report_FINAL.pdf, p. 63.

18 Topol, E. (2015) *The Patient Will See You Now* (Basic Books).

19 Angrist, M. and Cook-Deegan, R. (2014), Distributing the Future: The Weak Justifications for Keeping Human Genomic Databases Secret and the Challenges and Opportunities in Reverse Engineering Them', *Applied and Translational Genomics* 3: 124–127.

20 https://www.washingtonpost.com/news/the-intersect/wp/2016/08/19/98-personal-data-points-that-facebook-uses-to-target-ads-to-you/?utm_term=.10406a049780.

21 Facebook Financial Report September 2016, at https://s21.q4cdn.com/399680738/files/doc_financials/2016/Q3/3.-Facebook-Reports-Third-Quarter-2016-Results.pdf.

22 Topol, E. (2015) *The Patient Will See You Now* (Basic Books).

23 Peppet, S. R. (2014) 'Regulating the Internet of Things: First Steps Toward Managing Discrimination, Privacy, Security and Consent', *Texas Law Review* 93: 85–174.

24 Prainsack, B. and Buyx, A. (2017) *Solidarity in Biomedicine and Beyond* (Cambridge University Press).

25 Prainsack, B. (2015) 'Three "H"s for Health – The Darker Side of Big Data', *Bioethica Forum* 8(2): 4–5.

26 Ebeling, M. F. E. (2016) *Healthcare and Big Data: Digital Spectres and Phantom Objects* (Palgrave Macmillan).

27 This is an idea currently being advanced by Barbara Prainsack that strongly accords with a similar model earlier proposed by Bronwyn Parry to compensate for use of collected plant,

animal and microbial bioinformation – as set out in the
conclusion of Parry, B. (2004) *Trading the Genome: Exploring the
Commodification of Bioinformation* (Columbia University Press).

Selected Readings

Chapter 1 opens by examining the early adoption of bioinformation in forensic science. For a highly accessible
introduction to the topic of criminal identification and anthropometry, see Cole, S. A. (2009) *Suspect Identities: A History of
Fingerprinting and Criminal Identification* (Harvard University
Press). For interesting introductions to the rise of genetics
and molecular biology, see Keller, E. F. (2000) *The Century of
the Gene* (Harvard University Press) and Kay, L. (2000) *Who
Wrote the Book of Life? A History of the Genetic Code* (Stanford
University Press). Kay's work provides a very useful discussion of how genetic sequences came to be viewed as a form
of information and what the limits of such conceptions are.
A useful overview of the rise of bioinformation as a resource
is provided in Leonelli, S. (2016) *Data-Centric Biology: A
Philosophical Study* (University of Chicago Press). Insights
into the range and scope of processes of bodily commodifica-
tion can be found in contributions to two edited collections:
Scheper-Hughes, N. and Wacquant, L. (2003) *Commodifying
Bodies* (Sage) and Waldby, C. and Mitchell, R. (2006) *Tissue
Economies* (Duke University Press), while Sunder-Rajan, K.
(2006) *Biocapital: The Constitution of Postgenomic Life*
(London, Duke), Rose, N. (2009) *The Politics of Life itself:
Biomedicine, Power, and Subjectivity in the Twenty-First Century*
(Princeton University Press) and Cooper, M. E. (2011) *Life
as Surplus: Biotechnology and Capitalism in the Neoliberal Era*
(University of Washington Press) offer a critical consideration

of the political implications of this process. The case of the retention of children's organs without consent in UK hospitals is discussed in detail in Parry, B. (2013) 'The Afterlife of the Slide: Exploring Emotional Attachment to Artefactualised Bodily Traces', *History and Philosophy of the Life Sciences* 35(3): 431–447.

Chapter 2 focuses on the idea of provenance and how this shapes the production of collections of bioinformation in the form of biobanks. A good introduction to the issues surrounding the creation of biobanks is provided by Kaye, J. and Martin, P. (1999) *The Use of Biological Sample Collections and Personal Medical Information in Human Genetics Research* (Wellcome Trust). Several edited collections also provide useful examples of different kinds of biobanks and the ethical, legal and social issues they raise, including Tutton, R. and Corrigan, O. (2004) *Genetic Databases: Social and Ethical Issues in the Collection and Use of DNA* (London: Routledge) and Häyry, M., Chadwick, R., Árnason, V. and Árnason, G. (eds) (2007) *The Ethics and Governance of Human Genetic Databases* (Cambridge University Press). For more insight into the debates about Iceland's Health Sector Database, see Greenhough, B. (2006) 'Decontextualised? Dissociated? Detached? Mapping the Networks of Bioinformatics Exchange', *Environment and Planning A* 38(3): 445–463; Pálsson, G. and Rabinow, P. (1999) 'Iceland: The Case of a National Human Genome Project', *Anthropology Today* 15(5): 14–18; Rose, H. (2001) *The Commodification of Bioinformation: The Icelandic Health Sector Database* (Wellcome Trust); and Fortun, M. (2008) *Promising Genomics: Iceland and deCODE Genetics in a World of Speculation* (University of California Press). For an excellent critical overview of the Human Genome Diversity Project, see M'Charek, A. (2005) *The Human Genome Diversity Project: An Ethnography of Scientific Practice* (Cambridge University Press); for insights into the issues effecting indigenous populations, see Kowal, E. (2013) 'Orphan DNA: Indigenous Samples, Ethical Biovalue and Postcolonial Science', *Social Studies of Science* 43(4): 577–597. A detailed consideration of the issues surrounding the collection and use of forensic data can be found in Nuffield Council on Bioethics (2008) *The Forensic Use of Bioinformation: Ethical Issues*, at http://nuffieldbioethics.org/wp-content/uploads/The-forensic-use-of-bioinformation-ethical-issues.pdf; see also Wallace, H. M., Jackson, A. R., Gruber, J. and Thibedeau, A. D. (2014) 'Forensic DNA Databases – Ethical and Legal Standards: A Global Review', *Egyptian Journal of Forensic Sciences* 4(3): 57–63.

Chapter 3 explores the question of who owns bioinformation, and opens with a consideration of the competing public and private interests in mapping the human genome. For an introduction into the issues and debates surrounding the Human Genome Project, see Kevles, D. J. and Hood, L. (1993) *Code of Codes: Scientific and Social Issues in the Human Genome Project* (Harvard University Press) and Cook-Deegan, R. (1994) *The Gene Wars: Science, Politics and the Human Genome* (Norton). For insights into the process of turning bodily derivatives into scientifically and commercial valuable commodities, see Landecker, H. (2010) *Culturing Life* (Harvard University Press); Parry, B. (2006) 'New Spaces of Biological Commodification: The Dynamics of Trade in Genetic Resources and "Bioinformation"', *Interdisciplinary Science Review* 31(1): 19–31; and Sherkow, J. S. and Greely, H. T. (2015) 'The History of Patenting Genetic Material', *Annual Review of Genetics* 49(1): 161–182. We use a number of classic case studies to illustrate attempts to exert property rights over bioinformation. For more on the John Moore case, see Waldby, C. and Mitchell, R. (2006) *Tissue Economies: Blood, Organs, and Cell Lines in Late Capitalism* (Duke University Press), p. 88–109. For a compelling account of the HeLA cell lines, see Skloot, R. (2010) *The Immortal Life of Henrietta Lacks* (Crown Publishing Group). For more on the case of the Hagahai people of Papua New Guinea, see Kirsh, S. (2004) 'Property Limits: Debates on the Body in Nature and Culture', in Hirsch, E. and Strathern, M. (eds) *Transactions and Creations: Property Debates and the Stimulus of Melanesia* (Berghahn), pp. 21–39. For an influential critical account of some of the more general debates over intellectual property and indigenous rights, see Shiva, V. (1999) *Biopiracy: The Plunder of Nature and Knowledge* (South End Press). Finally, for insights and perspectives on the Myriad case, see Baldwin, A. L. and Cook-Deegan, R. (2013) 'Constructing Narratives of Heroism and Villainy: Case Study of Myriad's BRACAnalysis® Compared to Genentech's Herceptin®', *Genome Medicine* 5(8): 1–14; Cho, M. (2010) 'Patently Unpatentable: Implications of the Myriad Court Decision on Genetic Diagnostics', *Trends in Biotechnology* 28(10): 548–551; Matloff, E. T. and Brierley, K. L. (2010) 'The Double-Helix Derailed: The Story of the BRCA Patent', *The Lancet* 376(9738): 314–315; and Paradise, J. (2004) 'European Opposition to Exclusive Control Over Predictive Breast Cancer Testing and the Inherent Implications for US Patent Law and Public Policy: A Case Study of the Myriad Genetics' BRCA Patent Controversy', *Food & Drug Law Journal* 59(10): 132–154.

Chapter 4 explores the question of who benefits from the production, circulation and exploitation of bioinformation, beginning with the work of Nancy Wrexler and her search for the gene linked to Huntingdon's disease. See also the work of Nancy's sister, Alice Wexler (1996) *Mapping Fate* (California University Press), which is a compelling personal memoir of this search, and which provides an accessible introduction to both the science of gene discovery and the personal ethical challenges posed by the possibility of genetic testing. On the commercialization and privatization of bioinformational resources, see Lock, M. (2003) 'The Alienation of Body Tissues and the Biopolitics of Immortalised Cell Lines', in Scheper-Hughes, N. and Wacquant, L. (eds) *Commodifying Bodies* (Sage); and Parry, B. (2004) *Trading the Genome* (Columbia University Press). Rabinow, P. (1999) *French DNA: Trouble in Purgatory* (University of Chicago Press) offers insight into the issues raised around public–private collaborations in bioinformatics research; in a series of case studies, Rabinow explores the implications of the market in bioinformation for different groups and the ways in which bioinformation may be put to use. Read more about BiDil and the issues raised by racially targeted drug treatments in Brody, H. and Hunt, L. M. (2006) 'BiDil: Assessing a Race-Based Pharmaceutical', *Annals of Family Medicine* 4(6): 556–560; Pollock, A. (2012) *Medicating Race: Heart Disease and Durable Preoccupations with Difference* (Duke University Press). For further information on the possible forensic uses of bioinformation, see M'charek, A. (2008) 'Silent Witness, Articulate Collective: DNA Evidence and the Inference of Visible Traits', *Bioethics* 22(9): 519–528. Finally, we address the question of who benefits from the exploitation of bioinformation. A useful overview of benefit sharing is found in Simm, K. (2005) 'Benefit-Sharing: An Inquiry Regarding the Meaning and Limits of the Concept in Human Genetic Research', *Genomics, Society and Policy* 1(2): 29–40. Fortun, M. (2008) *Promising Genomics: Iceland and deCODE Genetics in a World of Speculation* (University of California Press) offers a critical perspective on deCODE's Health Sector Database and the benefits it may – or may not – bring to the Icelandic community. For useful insights into debates around bioinformation collected from indigenous populations, see Kowal, E. (2013) 'Orphan DNA: Indigenous Samples, Ethical Biovalue and Postcolonial Science', *Social Studies of Science* 43(4): 577–597; and Reardon, J. and TallBear, K. (2012) '"Your DNA Is Our History"':

Genomics, Anthropology, and the Construction of Whiteness as Property', *Current Anthropology* 53(S5): S233–S245.

Chapter 5 addresses the emergence of 'big data' and its influence on the production, circulation and exploitation of bioinformation. For an introduction to the scope and challenges posed by the 'big data' revolution in bioinformation, see Leonelli, S. (2016) *Data-Centric Biology: A Philosophical Study* (University of Chicago Press); Mittelstadt, B. and Floridi, L. (2016) *The Ethics of Biomedical Big Data* (BeSpringer); Kitchin, R. (2014) *The Data Revolution: Big Data, Open Data, Data Infrastructures and Their Consequences* (Sage). Shorter reflections on big data and its impact can also be found in *New Scientist* (2014) *Big Data, Better Health*, at https://www.newscientist.com/article/dn28340-big-data-be tter-health/; Marx, V. (2013) 'Biology: The Big Challenges of Big Data', *Nature* 498(7453): 255–260; Leonelli, S. (2014) 'What difference Does Quantity make? On the Epistemology of Big Data in Biology', *Big Data & Society* 1(1), DOI:https:// doi.org/10.1177/2053951714534395. To better understand the role that biobanks may play in realizing the goal of personalized medicine, see European Science Foundation (2012) *Personalised Medicine for the European Citizen*, at http:// archives.esf.org/coordinating-research/forward-looks/biom edical-sciences-med/current-forward-looks-in-biomedical-sc iences/personalised-medicine-for-the-european-citizen.html. On the process of 'prosumption', see Lupton, D. (2014) 'The Commodification of Patient Opinion: The Digital Patient Experience Economy in the Age of Big Data', *Sociology of Health and Illness* 36(6): 856–869. For a critical discussion of some of the implications of the big data revolution for healthcare, see Joyner, M. J., Paneth, N. and Ioannidis, J. P. A. (2013) 'What Happens When Underperforming Big Ideas in Research Become Entrenched?' *Journal of the American Medical Association* 316(13): 1355–1356; Van Horn, J. D. and

Toga, A. W. (2014) 'Human Neuroimaging as a "Big Data" Science', *Brain Imaging and Behavior* 8(2): 323–331; Bender, E. (2015) 'Big Data in Biomedicine', *Nature* 527(7576): S1–S1. For a detailed analysis of the implications of the racial stratification of medicines, see Inda, J. X. (2014) *Racial Prescriptions: Pharmaceuticals, Difference and the Politics of Life* (Routledge); Kahn, J. (2013) *Race in a Bottle: The Story of BiDil and Racialized Medicine in a Post-Genomic Age* (Columbia University Press) and Reardon, J. (2009) *Race to the Finish: Identity and Governance in an Age of Genomics* (Princeton University Press). For more on the risks to individual data privacy posed by biobanks, see Hoeyer, K. (2008) 'The Ethics of Research Biobanking: A Critical Review of the Literature', *Biotechnology and Genetic Engineering Reviews* 25: 429–452; Mittelstadt, B. D. & Floridi, L. (2016) 'The Ethics of Big Data: Current and Foreseeable Issues in Biomedical Contexts', *Science and Engineering Ethics* 22(2): 303–341; Parry, B. (2005) 'From the Corporeal to the Informational: Exploring the Scope of Benefit Sharing Agreements and their Applicability to Sequence Databases', in Theile, F. and Ashcroft, R. E. (eds) *Bioethics in a Small World* (Springer), pp. 73–91.

Finally, Chapter 6 explores bioinformatics futures. For an overview of the growth of bioinformatic resources and how these compare to other 'big data' sets, see Stephens, Z. D., Lee S. Y., Faghri, F., Campbell, R. H., Zhai, C., Efron, M. J., et al. (2015) 'Big Data: Astronomical or Genomical?' *Public Library of Science Biology* 13(7): e1002195. For more on the legacies of the Myriad case, see Conley, J. M., Cook-Deegan, R. and Lázaro-Muño, G. (2014) 'Myriad after Myriad: The Proprietary Data Dilemma', *North Carolina Journal of Law and Technology* 15(4): 597–637. For reflections on 'big data' futures, see Mayer-Schönberger, V. and Cukier, K. (2013) *Big Data: A Revolution That Will Transform How We Live, Work and Think* (John Murray) and Ebeling, M. F. E. (2016) *Healthcare and Big Data:*

Digital Specters and Phantom Objects (Palgrave Macmillan). For reflections on the darker side of big data, see Prainsack, B. (2015) 'Three "H"s for Health – The Darker Side of Big Data', *Bioethics* 8(2): 4–5. A more hopeful vision of the future, which sees prosumption and the datafication of everything as a 'democratization' of medicine, can be found in Topol, E. (2015) *The Patient Will See You Now* (Basic Books). For more on how we might govern bioinformation in the future, see Winickoff, D. and Winickoff, R. (2003) 'The Charitable Trust as a Model for Genomic Biobanks', *New England Journal of Medicine* 349(12): 1180–1184; and Prainsack, B. (2017) *Solidarity in Biomedicine and Beyond* (Cambridge University Press).

Index